BAMBOO and Barbed Wire

Stanley Wood-Higgs

ROMAN PRESS LIMITED
BOURNEMOUTH

ISBN 0 9503884 3 2

Published and printed in England by
Roman Press Limited, Bournemouth

Contents

The Author in 1941 just before going overseas

Foreword

I HAD intended writing a book about my captivity as soon as I had safely returned home but in the six months leave I had then, with nerves shot to pieces from our experiences, and the business of acclimatising to family life again, the impetus disappeared. Then pressures of the workaday world, the office and a dozen and one domestic demands kept it all in the background.

When I finally got around to getting it together I found I had an embarrassment of material. I had written some little books whilst still a prisoner; composed some verses and doggerel; made sketches; kept copies of what seemed important papers. I had acquired some possibly confidential documents including the 'Official Report on the Medical Aspect of Conditions prevailing . . . in Thailand and Burma': 'Transcripts from the Annual Medical Reports of the Prisoner of War Camp Changi from 15th February 1942 to 15th February 1945' and others. I had also in the years between read the few books already written by my fellow prisoners and innumerable newspaper articles. I had kept a diary whilst a prisoner; I had written short stories on my return to England.

So I had enough material for a weighty text book style publication, but by careful weeding and selection; very little editing and the writing of some connecting and explanatory paragraphs I have arrived at this book. My thanks to all those who have helped, some of them perhaps unwittingly; especially to my wife June, for having prodded me into doing it, and my daughter Catherine, for voluntarily typing out from the hot-potch of scraps of paper.

Although this was intended to be a Prisoner-of-War book, with emphasis on the Burma Death Railway, it seems to me that before one can write about being a Prisoner-of-War, one has to write about a War, and how one happens to be stupid enough to get in it. So perhaps this story starts, not on 15th February 1942 when I became a prisoner, but on 4th April 1939 when I joined the 162nd East Anglian Field Ambulance of the Royal Army Medical Corps (Territorial Army) at Harrow.

It is a long time ago — indeed a generation and more and there are some who say we should not drag up the past or lick over old wounds. On the other hand the War was *the* happening of the twentieth century and will be the central event of those hundred years which future historians will recognise as Sir Winston Churchill put it as the 'hinge of fate' which connected all that had gone before and all that was to come.

The War was global, almost total; it involved vast arsenals of weapons and horrifying new inventions; a broad sweep of canvas to paint the battles on; battles by land, sea and air. But the battles were fought by armies, and the armies consisted of corps, and they of Divisions, and they of units, and at the very lowest end was the individual — who sometimes wondered what it was all about, but mostly fixed his (or her) mind on the certainty that there must come an end — a time when they would 'Sound the Last All Clear'.

This is therefore the story, in part only, of one such individual — the tiniest bit of grit in one of the smallest working parts, of the little mechanism, that served the machine, that operated the Gargantua of War.

1 *Going to War 1939*

Train to Thailand

THE steel doors had rumbled along their grooves and been shut tight only two or three minutes before. Already the sun's heat on the roof and side had raised the temperature to a point almost unbearable. The combination of the growing heat in the box car goods van and the awful stench went past the point of being tolerable. I closed my eyes, drew my feet closer to my body, ignored the dull ache beginning in my skinny buttocks, and closed my eyes.

I did not sleep; yet I was not fully awake or aware of things around me; like so many other prisoners who had experienced depths of terror and despair which they could never have previously imagined, I had an inbuilt system or psyche which enabled me to shut out about three quarters of the real world.

The stench came from the twenty-six men in the rail wagon. In age from twenty to fifty; some diseased with dysentery or tropical sores or incipient malaria; all vastly under-nourished — correction — more than half-starved; little if any fat or even muscle left to protect bones from skin, or skin from steel plates. The Black Hole of Calcutta must have been something like this. Ten men might have, with adequate furnishings, such as a simple blanket, made the best of that truck. As it was, only half could sit or crouch, as I was while the other half stood or leaned, except the two in the middle who had already succumbed to their own diseases and the horrifying semi-darkness in that oven-hot cess-pit.

My head reeled; in the forlorn hope of sleep and my spirit seemed to leave me. How — in God's name, had I got there?

* * * * *

I had been convinced since Chamberlain came back from Munich in the late Autumn of 1938 that we were going to have a War, and that the best thing to do was to get into a unit of the army with some training before the War started, and so perhaps have a more comfortable War than one would otherwise have. Unfortunately in the six months that I tried to get into voluntary units I found that the Royal Artillery, the Royal Engineers and even Infantry Units were not taking any more recruits at that time into the Territorial Army. Eventually I went to the 162nd East Anglian Field Ambulance at South Harrow, where I lived, which was after all not perhaps so inappropriate since I was at the time working at the British Medical Association and had always been very interested in medical matters.

It was a very elite unit in that there was no member of it who had not matriculated at school, and there were many with University Degrees. How this happened I do not know but it did mean there was competition for any kind of promotion. It was certainly a question of the best among equals. More by luck than choice I was sent on a fortnight's course to the Army's School of Hygiene in Aldershot, and came away with a Distinction and therefore was immediately rewarded with that first rung on the ladder, the stripe of the Lance Corporal, which as anyone in the army will tell you amounts to almost nothing, but means an awful lot. All territorial units in those days went to an annual training camp and on 29th July 1939 we went to ours at Dibgate near Folkestone in Kent.

On the unfortunate illness of the Corporal in charge I received a further promotion and was put in charge of the 'Sanitary Squad' whose main job was to clean and keep clean the latrines throughout the camp — not particularly an elevating occupation, but one which enabled its holders to avoid irritating things like route marches and other kinds of fatigues.

Tension in Europe due to the insistent demands of Germany increased and on 1st September General Mobilisation was ordered. It was at that time a rule that the Territorial Army would immediately report for duty on General Mobilisation. It was with a considerable amount of satisfaction that a friend with whom I worked, and I, marched into our Chief Clerk's Office and told him we were away to the Wars, and that we would see him afterwards, knowing that the law said that our jobs had to be held for us.

Of course in the usual way, having reported to my local drill hall in full uniform, with gas mask and kit bag and the rest of it, it was found that they were not ready to receive us and we were sent away again for a night.

War was declared on 3rd September 1939 at 11 a.m. and within minutes the air raid sirens were sounded and although we could not credit that the Germans could be so quick off the mark we nevertheless took the precaution of taking cover — but in our case alongside a gasometer — would you believe!

Movement around the country and promotion to Sergeant followed, so that from that time until January 1940 the unit occupied three different headquarters and by Christmas Day 1939 were lodged in the drill hall of the 4th Norfolk Regiment at Framlingham.

On 11th January 1940 a new unit the 197 Field Ambulance was formed and the old 162 took unto itself a new RSM. A cadre of some fifteen officers and other ranks went to form the nucleus for the new unit, each of them receiving promotion, and I became a Staff-Sergeant.

The 197 advance party moved on January 15th to a new headquarters in Kings Lynn in Norfolk, standing in its own grounds, the home of the Dowager Lady Down, Hillington Hall. The task was to train 'intakes' of 'army classes' — euphemistic name for conscripts, because by that time conscription had begun and the task was to train (from P.T. first thing in the morning to lights out) — civilians into soldiers in the first place and then into medical orderlies or whatever the men were to become. On 23rd March 1940 I was promoted to Warrant Officer Class II Quarter Master Sergeant.

The unit later moved to places such as an encampment which was designed to become a Prisoner-of-War Camp for our enemies at Cranwich near Mundford in Norfolk, and then later to Lynford Hall. Later a move was made to Hethersett near Norwich, and then back again to Lynford Hall where a hospital was established.

On 8th January 1941 the unit moved out of England into Scotland to Lauder in Berwickshire and there carried out some intensive exercises in extremely cold and difficult circumstances. There were constant changes in the unit and just to complicate matters the army moved the 197th Field Ambulance on 11th April 1941 out of Lauder into Walsall, Staffordshire, and we were then trained for tropical warfare.

To digress a little, whilst we had been in Hethersett in Norfolk I had formed a dance band. Musicians, except perhaps pianists, tend to take their instruments with them, particularly under Service conditions, so that it was not surprising to hear groups of men singing to the music of one instrument or another. In this way I tracked down Driver Ken Dykins of the R.A.S.C. attached to the unit, playing piano with supreme skill, but without any knowledge of the theory of music or written notes. I think it was Corporal Bob Mills who played a piano accordion, and Private Joe Biggs R.A.M.C. with a fine set of drums which he certainly knew how to handle. I 'put in odd bits' on a B♭ clarinet and later an E♭ alto Saxophone which the unit bought for me. Because of my rank I suppose, certainly not because I was any the better musician, I found I was in charge. The Commanding Officer gave his approval and helped the band on many occasions.

We made up a name for the band out of the initials of the R.A.M.C. and R.A.S.C. of which a Field Ambulance is mostly formed and became the RAMSACS and drifted without realising it into using 'Whispering' as our signature tune.

We moved back to Lyndford Hall and held a couple of impressive dances in the ballroom and then in Lauder for weeks on end, in very cold weather, we held weekly dances in the village hall, even by popular demand having a go at traditional Scottish dances, helped considerably

THE RAMSACS

197th Field Ambulance Dance Band 1941
on stage at Penkridge

Pat, Bob, Doc, Joe, Bert (died 1944), *Arthur, Ken* (died May 1943), *Stan* (The Author)

by a local piper. So from Scotland back to the Midlands, Walsall, which was a cultural desert for us, and then shortly to a village called Penkridge.

The 'camp' at Penkridge was a street of semi-detached houses, recently built, some not yet finished, and none previously occupied. What were to be the back gardens became the parade ground and the community spirit blossomed in such an environment.

In those days villages such as this were crying out for entertainment close at hand, since travel was difficult, and we soon found ourselves providing dances, and indeed half of a full three hours' concert. The local A.R.P. had a strong entertainments organisation under a Mr. Richardson who worked with me on the organisation of the show. Thereafter we played for regular weekly dances, there and in other places. A vocalist was found for the band items in the show and retained — in the form of a young replacement Lieutenant Snell. A second accordionist was discovered, Private Arthur Preston and finally Private Reg Burrell who was a natural trumpeter. There could have been big things in store for the Band had we stayed there but we were drafted overseas.

We were paraded with 55 Brigade, part of the 18th Division for inspection by King George VI and we went by train to Liverpool on

29th October 1941. So by army lorry through interminable streets, with evidence of German aerial activity, to the Huskisson Wharf where awaiting our arrival (we were the last on board) was the 'Warwick Castle' a liner converted to troop carrying.

The cabin which I shared with three others was the civilian first class. The three others were Harry Hall (always called Henry) Sid Livesey, (the two R.A.M.C. Sergeants who were 'trooping' with me) and the odd spot, a Company Sergeant Major with whom we had nothing in common, and whom we promptly christened with a thoroughly rude nickname, which was so absolutely army in nature that it neither could be used in front of him nor repeated here.

I, and the two sergeants had been 'detached' from the main unit in order to go 'trooping' on another ship with another unit of combatant troops. We had about ten other members of the Field Ambulance, two doctors, two corporals and the rest nursing orderlies. Perhaps a word of explanation on what is known as 'trooping' in the Medical Corps is necessary here. When a ship containing combatant troops and other personnel was sent abroad (in those days at least) a unit of the RAMC went with them, or part of a unit, in order to care medically for them, and this was the purpose of our being on the Warwick Castle and divorced from our own Field Ambulance. We had in fact on board a battalion of the 9th Royal Northumberland Fusiliers who were a tough bunch but who, as all soldiers do, treated the knowledge if not the persons of members of the Medical Corps with considerable respect.

So out into Mersey mouth and under our own steam up the west coast of Britain until we were informed that the line of blue hills in the distance was on Caledonian soil. Here we picked up the rest of the convoy and slowly sorting ourselves into formation there appeared, like grey guardian angels the watchdogs of the Atlantic — the Navy. Not, from the point of view of an enemy a formidable force, but so far as we were concerned adequate against anything less than a Grand Fleet. Our course appeared to be westward and rumour, so rife on board ship, immediately raised some twenty possibilites in regard to the port on the seaboard of the American continent at which we would eventually arrive.

One grey and very dreary morning as I was leaning across the rail of the upper deck in my usual early morning attempt to dispel the overheated air which was the atmosphere of the ship, there was a slight swell and a fine drizzle of rain, but not sufficient to render being outdoors unpleasant. The other ships of our convoy were readily discernible and in the haze beyond them, on the skyline, the escorting warships that had left England with us — a handful of small ships of the Royal Navy. Out of the spindrift to the westward appeared more and more ships. The British ships turned, our convoy of transports kept steadily on, the Navy escort took over control of the eastbound ships and their own escort turned in towards us, followed and caught us up, and went with us.

We knew we had been handed and taken over deliberately, but why was another matter. These ships were American — plainly flying the Stars and Stripes — some small, some large. Included among them was an aircraft carrier from the deck of which shortly appeared (to clinch the argument with those who doubted) a flight of planes with stars on the lower sides of their wings, wheeling and dipping above our ships.

Did we but know it we were making history, since America was by no means in the War at that time.

2 *A Long Cruise 1941*

Reverie on the train

THE train jolted and stopped suddenly. I came back from my reverie of what seemed by contrast to be halcyon days. There had been some good times, some full bellies and sensual moments, some experiences to be enjoyed, treasured and remembered.

Now there was only the suffocating heat, the smells, the awful pain in the pelvic bones which made it a pleasure to be standing, but an agony to get upright; my half hour had passed — now it was my turn to stand — and something was happening outside. There was noise, shouting, even the distant chunk-chunk of the engine exhaust. The bolts or bars outside the sliding door on one side of the wagon were released. The door slid back. A Japanese (or possibly a Korean) stood outside with a fixed bayonet and shouted at us to get out — laced with 'kurra-kurra' and other odd mixtures of Nippon and English sounds. We got out and saw the length of the train, mostly in front of us, and most of us hastily joined our comrades at the side of the track with our shorts down, squatting, gaining temporary relief from the cramping diarrhoea pains we all had. Luckier men simply needed to urinate, or even managed to smoke the revolting stalk-like rubbish we called tobacco. Of course the sun still shone brassily, but these few miles out of Singapore, somewhere at the toe of Johore, there was a little breeze.

Already the perpetual arguing and haggling with the guards had begun again. The more senior of us protested at the conditions in the wagons — could not the sick be moved — could not the doors be left open? See! It was possible to fasten them so that there was a three-inch gap, which even in our emaciated state we could not pass through.

The engine whistle sounded. Another train rumbled by on the through line past the loop on which ours was standing — the reason for the stop. Get back in! Stop arguing! Kurra! — clang, and the door was closed; the train started with a fierce jerk, and made confusion worse confined inside the wagons.

Wearily I leaned against the side, a tiny draught from some interstice in the ancient metal allowing air in. In seconds torpor had descended on me again . . .

* * * * *

So eventually we came into the port of Halifax — the first overseas port to touch — albeit we had seen Iceland in the distance when we were in mid-ocean. We waited tied up for the day and as dusk fell stepped on to the land of New Scotland — for two hundred yards only — and then through the dimly-lit wharf to American soil in the shape of our next ship. The U.S. Transport 'Orizaba'.

As night fell — to our eyes accustomed to the black-outs of England there came as a welcome relief the star-spangling lights of a non-belligerent town. We leaned by hundreds on the rails of our respective ships and watched them flicker and wink, while arc-lights on the quayside lit up as day, the loading and unloading operations.

For myself, I found the American at that time, not a little patronising in his manner to the English. This attitude was borne out too by the older men, whose chief slogan seemed to be that 'they' had won the last war for us and did not see why either they, or America should get us 'out of this'. Many and long were the arguments we had as to the relative merits and demerits of Britain, America, their respective navies and armies, Communism, the Democrats and Republicans, Conservatism and the British Monarchy. They confessed that a lot of our idiom was strange and unintelligible to them but none of them exceeded in gall the remark made to me on one occasion. I was talking about the coronation ceremony and the remark was made by a typical 'Bowery' tough whose tongue I will endeavour to represent. His first effort was an attack (vitriolic in the extreme) against my Oxford accent (which I do not have) followed by the words "Why don't youse guys shpeak Inglish, so's oder guys kin unnerstan' yer," — this in a hoarse gangster voice.

U.S.S. Orizaba — 5,000 tons pre-1914 vessel

Life on shipboard very rapidly became a matter of routine and slightly easier relations established. Everything on the ship was regulated by bosun's whistles and announcements made over a public address system. One announcement which will live with me all my days was heard after reveille was sounded over the ship's intercom system every morning. It went something like this. "Now hear this, sweepers man your brooms, clean sweep down fore and aft, empty all trash cans."

We slipped down the east coast of the American continent, albeit out of sight of land, and the weather became steadily warmer; our khaki drill (tropical kit) was hauled out of its hibernation and a crop of bare white knees and pinky arms made its appearance.

Our escort on this stage of the trip is worthy of mention. The Americans evidently did not think it wise to leave anything to chance and on this account we had an embryo battle fleet as our escort; I counted at least two cruisers, an aircraft carrier and a large bevy of destroyers. The ships actually in convoy were few — six in fact. They were, in order of tonnage: 'The West Point', 'Wakefield', Mount Vernon', 'Leonard Wood', 'J.T. Dickman', and far and away the most insignificant my own home, the 'Orizaba'. We were joined after Trinidad by an oil tanker, but more of that later. Our two days' stay in Trinidad was somewhat of an event. This was the first port to be regarded as 'overseas' as well as the first occasion upon which our khaki drill made a public appearance.

In some strange way Halifax was too common knowledge to be taken seriously, and the crossing of the Atlantic, too prosaic to be regarded as an adventure; but here, life as it was lived in the Empire overseas, and the meaning of Britain's vast commonwealth of nations, first burst upon me. Everything one could see from the rail of the ship (how often that barrier presented itself!) was new; palm trees, negroes, native policemen, the ubiquitous khaki drill of our overseas forces; shouting and screaming of natives and their peddling of wares; in the foreground the dock sheds with their multifarious activities and leaden colour. We did stay for one day tied up in Sobo for the purpose of oiling, but apart from an intriguing view of a native settlement the vista consisted mostly of pipes and tanks, and we were not allowed ashore.

So on the 22nd we left Trinidad for the next stage of the journey which was probably the most exciting of the voyage. In the first place we were at sea, that is out of sight of land, for a period of three weeks. Furthermore, we became, day by day, an easier prey to enemy submarines which we well knew to be operating from a base at Dakar. As time went on our medical work became harder.

On the Warwick Castle things had been very easy because of the unrestricted facilities we had, and because the crew were English. Here things were different. We had to share the use of the Medical Inspection room with the Americans, and all our dispensary requirements were met by them entirely. We did have however, the advantage of the use of an X-ray apparatus and laboratory equipment.

The daily routine was as follows: Soon after the published time for breakfast, a parade of the daily sick was held and each man seen in turn by our duty M.O., either Capt. Cormack, or (as he was then) Lt. Chester. The names were first entered by our clerk, and the men marshalled into something like an orderly mass by Sgt. Hall, who combined this duty with that of interpreter of the two languages represented by the English and the American pharmacopiae. The patient was seen by the M.O. who diagnosed, prescribed and ordered him to return on a certain day. This information was written on to a prescription chit duly bowdlerised and edited and the patient, plus chit passed on to Sgt. Livesey and his satellite nursing orderlies for treatment. A treatment parade was held in the afternoons and on occasions dental or other work done.

All the staff (apart from the M.Os — there were only fifteen of us including two batmen) actually tried their hand at almost anything there was to be done. In point of fact by the end of the voyage one had acquired a considerable amount of clinical experience about the minor ailments.

Off duty there was plenty to occupy the time. A daily newsheet was published which always gave a fruitful source for argument. Soon after we left Trinidad an oil tanker which had attached itself to the flotilla nosed alongside and some abortive attempts were made to get a hose across to us. The third attempt was successful however, and a derisive cheer went up from the watching troops.

We found ourselves, after two days out of Trinidad, rapidly approaching what is, we were told at school 'an imaginary line running round the earth' — the Equator. I suppose as landlubbers we all have at some time or other envisaged ourselves as the object of a crossing-the-line ceremony, and shivered in anticipation of being lathered, shaved, ducked and drubbed. Imagine though, the relief when we were told that owing to the strain of affairs, circumstantial to crossing an ocean not too healthy from the point of view of enemy aircraft and ships, the ceremony had been cancelled! So we crossed the line for the first time, and the mark of our crossing was an embellished certificate signed by the master of the ship to the effect that Davy Jones had enrolled us on the list of trusty 'Shellbacks'. Did we but know it we were to become very ancient 'members of the deep' before we were very much older. The 24th of November saw us in latitude 00.00 — neither north nor south!

So this long voyage across a waste of waters began. There were incidents which enlivened the daily routine. On more than one occasion a submarine scare would be felt by the ships in convoy and as a result 'action stations' would be rung on the ship's alarm and the destroyers would scurry off in a circle in an attempt to find the cause of the trouble. We sometimes saw founts of water but nothing more concrete than that.

In the evenings too, there were sometimes boxing or other spectacles to be watched on 'A' deck. When the blanket of night fell, instead of a hot stuffy cabin (mine was the smallest on the ship) one could lean on the rail. Watching the myriad points of phosphorescence flashing in the creamy wake of the prow, one could speculate on the immensity of the ocean and the uncertainty of the future; or some energetic spirit would bring out a musical instrument and lead the thronged decks in a sing-song, when one could sing loud and long to dispel morbid humours, soft and low and luxuriate in sentiment, or just lean and listen, lingering still in the pleasant past, and savouring in advance the thrill of the future.

On Sundays too, in the true British manner things had to be organised on a different basis. Church services were held with a hymn service in the evening. At almost all of the services I took part in, the music was provided by what was originally intended to be part of a dance band.

The change of months was ushered in by a typical storm in the 'roaring forties'. I had however managed to maintain, in the face of numerous patients who complained of the illness, a stony countenance to that landlubber's destiny, seasickness. The rough weather, just before we reached Cape Town, was a test for any man.

For two or three days the wind blew fiercely and all the ships tossed and rolled. Our own, little 'Orizaba', a mere cattleboat, did everything but stand on her head. There were moments, especially during the night when the M.I. room and numerous other places were wrecked by loose furniture, that I thought she was going to do even that.

I contrived to keep myself in my bunk, which was a top one, by the simple expedient of lashing a rope around the foot of the mattress and its supports, and a belt around my middle. My equilibrium (mental not physical) was upset however, by a plaintive call in the middle of the night for assistance at the now wrecked M.I. room. One of the men had fallen out of his bunk and landing against a supporting pillar below decks, had gashed hand and head fairly well. Large lashings of plaster however dealt with him till the morning when the M.O. could see him.

As November crept into December we knew, with the certainty with which one can know things on board ship that we were not only approaching the land mass of Africa, but what was much more exciting was that we were likely to make port at Cape Town. This to over a thousand soldiers who had been cooped up in a ship for nigh on three weeks was a foretaste of heaven. Our hopes were premature however. We ran so far south as to find it extremely cold on deck and only just warm enough in the cabin at nights. Furthermore, by furtive glimpses at the compass set aft of 'A' deck it appeared that we were literally going round in small circles.

In hindsight it is probably true that at that particular time no one knew quite what to do with us or our convoy.

EXTRACT FROM THE SECRET SESSION SPEECHES
OF MR. CHURCHILL

> 'I had obtained from President Roosevelt, in October last, shipping sufficient to carry two divisions additional to our ordinary heavy convoys from this country to the Middle East. The first of these divisions, the 18th, was rounding the Cape in the early days of December. It was destined for the Levant-Caspian front . . . Both these divisions were immediately diverted to the Malay Peninsula.'

It is true that the attitude of the Americans which had been patronising in the extreme suddenly changed on the 8th December when the news of the attack on Pearl Harbour by the Japanese was broadcast. Suddenly they wanted to know how we had coped with the War; and what was going on; and what did we think they would be doing and a much more friendly spirit immediately was felt. The continual wandering about the seas however, eventually came to an end and early one morning there appeared in the distance the outline of a coast.

On nearer acquaintance a characteristic flat-topped mountain became discernible and as the sun broke through the clouds we were able to see the famous Table Mountain — with the 'tablecloth' spread. There stretched before us the possibility of glorious days ashore, with money to spend and things to buy.

The first evening was undoubtedly remarkable. One had heard tales of the unlimited hospitality of the Cape people but it passed belief. Apart from the officially organised services such as the Y.M.C.A. and the Entertainments Committee of the town, it was apparent from the large number of private cars waiting at the dock gates that we were welcome.

Our wanderings took us through the Park and a quiet hotel advertising dinners, came into sight. With the greatest of pleasure Henry, Sid and myself entered and sat down. A glance at the menu readily decided for us that the typically English dinner which was one of the possibilities was the dinner for us, and to the waiter who appeared we expressed our wishes, having first asked, in the canny way common to soldiers the financial damage likely to accrue therefrom. He mumbled about the price and went off to some dark corner to find out. When he returned with the soup, he told us, in dialect I cannot hope to reproduce, that the proprietress of the hotel would be glad if we would dine at her expense. We protested, but only mildly.

When we left I made what I hope was a pretty speech thanking the good lady, who made it quite clear that British soldiers might do it at any time — it was her little contribution to the War Effort.

This was but the first surprise. We had no sooner emerged into the busy streets once more when a large and prosperous looking car pulled up and the driver, leaning out, asked if we would like a lift. We were highly suspicious, with the suspicion born in Englishmen by the 'Fifth column' scare; we were not impressed by the sumptuous car nor by its middle-aged male occupant; we decided that three were a match for one however and stepped in.

We were, during the rest of our stay in Cape Town, taken home, wined, dined and taken out in their car; shown the sights by day and night; driven to Muizenberg and Rondebosch and made to feel thoroughly at home. The comforts of home, combined with English food were pleasures appreciated as only we could then appreciate them. When we needed advice as to what to see and when to see it we were told. We listened to the News from London. We had a good time! One afternoon by dint of leaving the ship at the earliest possible moment, catching the bus to Kloof Nek before it became crowded, and taking the first 'mountain' bus to the lower cable station, Sid and I contrived to be the first among those who ascended Table Mountain by the cableway that afternoon.

I have not a good head for heights and I confidently expected to feel some distress on the journey. I felt very little; I was only amazed at the beauty of the mountainside, with its flowering shrubs and daintily coloured weeds and jubilant with the feeling that we were sailing into the clouds to a world far above the murmurs of war. With this impression we stepped out of the upward car and mingled with the others in purchasing mementoes of the trip. Then out on to the concrete promenade where the wind plucked with chilly fingers and wisps of cloud floated below or eddied around. We walked out over the top of the mountain which of course is far from flat, and choosing a sheltered spot, (one hundred and eighteen paces past the last pair of upright boulders, eighteen paces to the right of the path and down into a dip) we left 1941 halfpennies to be collected when next we were that way, and so far as I know they are still there.

We resumed our voyage and a British cruiser became our escort and the American warships turned back. We were grateful to them for their protection in the past six weeks — but we were very comfortable with our ship flying the Union Jack!

On the 20th of December, the 'Orizaba' turned west away from the convoy which was bound north, and after an interval of two days put in to the port of Mombasa. I think that not only was it necessary for refuelling purposes but also because of 'the exigencies of the military situation'. This was not apparent however, and here for the first time we experienced living ashore under tropical conditions.

Here again, we had a considerable amount of shore leave. We spent most of it at the 6th East African General Hospital — a hospital being conducted by part of the personnel of a South African Field Ambulance and a largish staff of East and South African nurses. Here too we experienced unlimited hospitality; bathing in the afternoons; drinks and dinner in the evening; the facilities of the Sergeants' Mess open to us and guides for the small amount of guiding we needed in the town.

Owing to my activities on board ship in the matter of the dance band, I was fortunate enough to have a late pass from the ship on Christmas night, in common with the other members of the band. This was to enable us to perform at Government House for a dance given by the Governor in honour of Christmas — a dance to which the military and naval officers of the two ships then lying in port, with a sprinkling from the newcomer ships, were invited. Partners were, if not plentiful, at least sufficient and the dance was voted a success. The Governor (I forget his name — my apologies!) was kind enough to ask the band back to a late supper at two in the morning at his Residence. Never did cold turkey, new bread, and beer taste more delicious.

The following night — Boxing night — Henry and I, after an abortive attempt to gatecrash the General Hospital party, and a drink in what appeared to be a somewhat shady hotel, had dinner in style at the Imperial Hotel. An excellent dinner through whose fourteen courses we waded with a grim relish. We drank heartily with each course, so that by the time we came to what was to be the last course, the fruit and nuts, we were both well gone. I remember the waiter — an incredibly elderly native whom we called 'boy', coming to the table with a bowl full of fruit, and Henry, by which time unable to remain on his chair, sliding gracefully down below the table, and just saving himself by his fingertips and his nose and peering over the edge, saying. "Wot no nuts."

We sailed again on 27th December 1941 and had a Watch Night Service on board for the New Year. Our next port was Bombay where we tied up alongside Ballard Pier on 5th January 1942.

3 *India*
1942

On a train to nowhere

I LOST count of the times I had stood, leaned, and transferred my weight from one leg to the other; or taken my turn for 'yasume' — the illusion of rest on that metal floor, and the bone bruise-laden rattling of the wheels.

When next the doors were opened, night had fallen although a clear, almost full moon, made the extra vigilance of the guards unnecessary.

Where could we escape to? The nearest friendly forces or even population could be hundreds and hundreds of miles away. To disappear into the scrub at the side of the line was only for natural reasons, not for the heinously wicked prisoner-of-war crime of escape. We moved the sick to a kind of passenger coach; we 'brewed up' with the dusty ration of so-called tea, and hot water straight from the engine boiler. We recovered from our rush to the bushes. We were allowed to lie down. Or rather we lay down and even the guards realised we were doing no harm to the Great East Asia Co-prosperity Sphere — and could do no harm in our condition, even if we cherished uncharitable thoughts. Some slept. I must have done . . .

* * * * *

Bombay was a town of smells, blanketed with an aura of perspiring oriental humanity, fresh fruit and bad drainage. We did a little shopping and the cry of 'Two anna backsheesh' was to become a very familiar one to us. In the Mahatma Ghandi Road — one of the main streets of Bombay, we were accosted by a pock-marked young woman, enveloped in a brilliant sari and carrying a small naked child. To the accompaniment of much gesticulation and patting the child's bare posterior she demanded backsheesh. Not content with this she partially disrobed and increased her excited gabblings. We laughed and reiterated the rather rude command to 'bugjao'. She, taking our laughter for acquiescence only redoubled her efforts. Finally she clung to Henry's arm to the great amusement of Sid and myself. We were by now in the middle of this very wide road and not a few pedestrians were interested in our appearance. I felt her clinging to my arm and thrusting the child at me, and crimson with embarrassment I shouted, "go away." My embarrassment turned to panic when I saw that Sid and

Henry had deserted me and were coldly walking along the nearer pavement. Eventually I rid myself of the woman and gave the baby to a policeman.

To get a good dinner we went to Green's Hotel — mostly because we had seen that they had a fine dance band dais and fancied music with our food. But when we got there, we did not exactly find the cupboard bare, but barred to us. The place was picketted by Military Police who were adamant in their refusal to admit us. I put on an air of authority however, claimed (justifiably) Warrant Officership and got us in.

Whilst we were there, one of the officers who was on our boat came in, accompanied by a slightly overdressed and slightly over made-up girl. They sat for their dinner and as they did so a friend of the officer went to their table and said. "Introduce me old man!"

The reply was. "Shertainly. Margaret meet Lt. Brown, Jimmy this is Miss — er — let me see what is your name?"

The next day we were sent to the Re-inforcement camp at Deolali, one of a choice of four. The others being: Colabar, Poona, and Ahmednagar. Now this is only a short train journey inland, but don't misunderstand the term. 'Short' in this part of the world is any distance up to three to four hundred miles. This was on the 7th January and for just seven days I was to be left in peace here. Life on the ship had not been too hard but it had been very wearying — the eternal procession of sick, lame and lazy palls very easily! This camp came as a pleasant respite.

The number of Indians in and around the camp was considerable. Apart from the population of the village (always known as the bazaar) there were the workmen, the boys who cleaned the Atapp huts in which we lived, (and ourselves if we let them), the fruit and tea 'wallahs' and the 'dhurzie' and 'dhobie' men — tailors and laundrymen.

Here we had our first experience of mosquito nets, and our first ride in a 'tongah' the hill equivalent of the 'gharrie'. The 'boy' permanently attached to the hut which was my temporary home, was an old fellow, of I suppose, sixty. Bearded and enveloped in a tremendous white garment, he had the appearance of a scorbutic and scrofulous patriarch. He was devoted to us, or at least appeared so, and we endeavoured to reward his devotion. We christened him early in life — Jim — a name to which he soon learned to respond. Here it was that we experienced what we had been told but found hard to believe, that these servants were so expert that they could come into your sleeping quarters, work there, and indeed even shave you while you still slept. This latter, I could not accept until one morning I woke to find myself shaven, having had no knowledge of it whatsoever. Maybe it had been a heavy night the night before.

Deolali, (spelled by the Indians — Devlali) is known to the army as 'Doolally' and it is from this place that the expression 'Doolally tap', meaning 'non compos mentis' originates. It grew apparently from a combination of the facts that at Deolali there is, or was, a home for mental defectives, who developed in the army, and from the continual tap, tap, made by the native stone breakers' hammers.

On the 17th of the month my rest was shattered. One of the majors of the Field Ambulance unit, which meanwhile was at Ahmednagar, came with a relief to replace me, and to take me back with him to the unit. The journey was quite an adventure. We had the usual first class coach with shower and lavatory attached, consisting of two sleeping berths, or rather bunks, only. We played chess, discussed the war; I reported on the trip out so far and he told me news of the unit; we slept a little; and we dined. Oh yes — we dined; and in state too; once again I tasted the far flung power of the British King Emperor.

It was this way. To get to Ahmednagar from Deolali one must change at Manmud (pronounced Mahnmood — to rhyme with 'good'). Before leaving Deolali we had rung Manmud (one hundred miles away) and ordered dinner for two — to be consumed in the half hour wait we had between connections. But our train arrived late and when we pulled into the junction we had in fact ten minutes only to spare. There was a waiter (Indian of course) on the platform and as ours was the only first class compartment on the train (and for that matter I believe we were the only Europeans) he readily found us. Shouting an order to the host of 'boys' clustered round he led us dexterously through the crowd, over a bridge, across some lines, up the side of the platform and into the dining room. Another appeared and whisked in front of us a delightful menu. Casting a regretful eye over it we decided that we should have to miss something like half of it when the 'Manager' for want of a better name, of the place hurried up and said that we were to eat just what we wanted. We were not to worry about catching the train, and he would see the station master about holding up the train.

At twelve minutes past the time appointed for that train to leave we clambered into another first class compartment, at that moment being dusted by a man who fondly hoped for backsheesh, and wherein already were reposing our numerous baggages.

Wars might go on, trains could have schedules, but nothing was allowed to come between the Englishman and his dinner in the days of the British Raj.

It was two in the morning and cold when we reached Ahmednagar. Ahmednagar was not as pleasant as Deolali but it was good to be back with the unit again. There was much handshaking all round the rather wondering glances from those who had not known I was arriving. I found a lot of changes not in the constitution of the unit but in the personalities of the men and officers. Some good, some bad; I suppose they saw a difference in me too.

Time off at Ahmednagar was spent mostly in sport. We had hockey, football, cricket, athletics and organised country walks — known to the uninitiated as route marches. So time went by, broken by occasional highlights, such as the weekly landing of the aeroplane on the sport's field, and the occasion when the Ramsacs (the unit dance band) played at the Fighting Vehicle School Sergeants' Mess Dance.

On the 22nd of January we left Ahmednagar, by march route as far as the station, by train into Bombay once again and within two hours on to the ship bearing us to what we supposed would be our ultimate destination. The ship was the 'Empress of Asia' and the destination we thought was either Singapore or Palestine.

The date of embarkation was the 23rd and the day was Friday. Nobody of course ever sails on a Friday — it's unlucky, or so everyone said; and I suppose they were right. At all events the R.S.M. and my friend Jack Sugg the transport Sergeant Major, myself and one of the Staff-Sergeants shared a reasonable cabin and the food was good.

S.S. Empress of Asia
Built 1913 — destroyed 1942 (see also Appendix)

4 *Under Fire*

Back to the train

IT WAS getting light. For a few seconds of half-waking half-sleeping life was good. The air was cool and pleasant, the ground unbelievably soft and there was the homesick smell of steam trains.

We were disturbed none too politely, herded to the river — the highly suspect stream a yard wide fifty yards away across the scrub. We rinsed. Again there was the trek to the engine to beg for hot water from the Indian driver, and back to make a drink of some kind.

Now to scramble back into that awful wagon. The sun suddenly in full view above the trees. There were slightly less of us now. One or two had been removed — to the 'sick' wagon. One was not accounted for. Nobody knew where he was. The 'tenko' had been perfunctory and we missed him only when making a conversational roll call. He was never heard of again. Did he just walk into the jungle and keep walking until he dropped from weakness, or a snake bite or even a Nippon bullet?

The door was left with a crack open. The night's cooling had warped the runners. It wouldn't move shut — we tried — just a little — but it stayed. The heat was as bad; the smell was as bad and we were traversing a more closely wooded part of the peninsula; there was a smell of woodsmoke. Suddenly I was back on that burning ship . . .

* * * * *

Up till now, both at home and overseas the unit had had a good time. Little was done beyond training, manoeuvres and the M.I. Room work for neighbouring battalions. We were to taste in this month however, the whole gamut of war — not I feel, in all the intensity which we may have been called upon to undergo but sufficient to bring us back from the artificial toy soldier existence we had been leading into the world of stern reality.

February 1942 came in with us somewhere in the Indian Ocean, south of India and west of the Dutch East Indies. We knew by now that our destination must be Singapore and we had heard on the ship's radio how the advancing Japanese had pushed the allies out of Johore across the Causeway to Singapore Island.

We had been overflown by Japanese planes almost every day while we were crossing the Indian Ocean. The 'Empress of Asia' was a coal-burning four-funnel vessel with a very high wooden superstructure. The stokers were Liverpool Irish and they went on strike in the middle of the Indian Ocean. The Royal Northumberland Fusiliers who were there, were made to be the stokers and of course they were inexperienced and incapable of doing the job properly, consequently we dropped back from the convoy; we were slow and were making something of the speed of five knots instead of possibly, ten, twelve or fifteen.

On the 3rd February I decided that in view of the possible approach of much action and the consequent proximity of my possible demise it would be advisable to write a 'last letter' and all that sort of thing. This I did and together with my photos and other small things of some sentimental value put them inside one of the Army's most useful pieces of equipment — the anti-gas wallet. The whole I tied, with great foresight, in my life jacket.

At twelve-thirty the following day I was sitting with Jack Sugg in the Sergeants' Mess lounge attempting to play German whist, when I was attracted by what appeared to be gunfire; Jack said. "Practising I expect." But as I turned to the window I saw a squadron of nine bombers flying in formation towards the ship.

I remember saying something about, "Is it — Hell!" as we both went for our steel helmets in the cabin. Ten yards from the cabin however, there was a swish and a roar, and another, and the ship shook from stem to stern. I found myself on the floor but after a lapse of a few minutes everything seemed quiet and I got to the cabin. Steel-helmetted and with my 'Mae West' tied around me I went to 'Action Stations' but after only ten minutes the 'All Clear' alarm bell sounded.

The next morning there came to our gladdened eyes a coastline which we were assured was that of Singapore. We were making very small speed. The alarm sounded and rather bewildered we accoutred ourselves, (our kits were all packed and stacked neatly in the cabin) and took up our positions; but ten minutes later the 'All Clear' went and I walked up to the deck. As I passed my cabin window I threw my steel helmet through. As I turned to lean on the rail I saw a flash from the guns of one of the cruisers with us; followed by the report and a cacophony of sound broke out. There was the roar of 'planes, chattering of machine guns, deep roar of big guns and the alarm bell. We hastened to our posts and then the fun began in earnest.

My post was with Captain Clarkson of the Dental Corps in a ward, three decks below the boat deck, which had been set aside for casualties from the lower decks. We were almost immediately hit, and the tinkle of breaking glass, combined with a red glow suggested that the saloon above our heads had been hit. The glow deepened and soon the ratings who were fighting it retreated down the stairs leading to the foyer, before the advancing flames. The hoses spewed out only a thin trickle of water totally inadequate for the purpose because of the lack of pressure due to bad firing below decks. The din went on; first one would hear the roar of the Ack Ack guns, then the rapid tapping of the .5 inch repeaters, and as the rat-a-tat of Brens and Tommy-guns joined in the chorus, there came the swish of bombs, their boom as they struck the water, or the juddering shock as the ship was hit. Again and again, for what must have been an hour the bombers returned; the other ships made Singapore, some of them damaged but we had to stay put because we had no steam.

The attack abated and it became clear from the heat in that lower ward and the paint dripping off the ceiling, that the fire above was of no mean dimensions. Then there came the order to abandon ship. All this while the casualties we had suffered were being treated at the various first aid posts and we first evacuated the patients we had. They went over the side tied to doors and stretchers hoping that they would keep upright.

When by a roundabout route I eventually emerged into the bright noonday sun a sight unforgettable met my eyes. All the upper works of the ship, from the promenade deck to the bridge and back for about half of the ship were ablaze. It was an old ship and she burned well! We crowded on to the fore part of the promenade deck, huddled together and crouching down to keep out of the way of falling sparks and because the bombers came back to machine-gun. They were driven off however, by heavy gunfire and a silence fell on those who like me, were standing on the narrow wedge of deck between the bridge and the bows. The ship had by now quite stopped and the port anchor dropped. The starboard anchor was still to go however, and the Captain of the Ship, The Officer Commanding Troops, I believe our own O.C. and a bevy of men including myself, released the chocks, and eased the chain over its first few links until the weight of the anchor told and it ran with a roar to the ocean bed.

The swimmers went over the starboard side to swim to a lighthouse some four hundred yards away while the non-swimmers went down a rope on the port side. They would not move however, whether through lack of faith in their life jackets or because they hoped to be taken off by one of the smaller vessels nosing alongside. Finally when the O.C. Troops asked someone to lead the way Jack and I said. "Come on," simultaneously and went.

Down the rope we went and I picked up a tiny burn inside my thigh. Fortunately even as a schoolboy I had had rope climbing instruction and so managed the way down to the bottom fairly easily.

KEY

A. Liverpool 29.10.41.
B. Halifax 8.11.41.
C. Trinidad 20.11.41.
D. 1st crossing-line 24.11.41.
E. Roaring Forties
F. Cape Town 9.12.41.
G. Mombasa 22.12.41.
H. 2nd crossing-line
I. Bombay 5.1.42 & 23.1.42.
J. 3rd crossing-line 25.1.42.
K. 4th crossing-line 4.2.42.
L. Bombing 4.2.42.
M. Firing of Empress of Asia

The first few minutes in the water were pleasant, since it had been hot on the deck and the water was simply cool. I struck out to get away from the ship and managed about thirty yards and found to my horror that the current was drawing me into the ship's side and I was still trying to swim when I felt something bump into my backside and found I was immediately beneath the stern and could see the propellers which were of course stationary. I remember the horror I experienced when I saw a boat fall from its davits and strike a man in the water beneath, and the sense of futility when I saw the flames roaring back past my cabin. I drifted away from the ship.

Once or twice I tried to make some other party or get on a raft but always it just floated by and I was beginning to shiver and I believe, talk to myself, when I saw a little gunboat bearing down upon me. It seemed at first as though he might run me down and I shouted and cursed and swore in an agony of apprehension, but a rope was thrown and I was hauled — I had no strength to climb — into the boat. I lay there panting for a few moments and then asked the time. I found I had been in the water unbelievably two hours and a half or more. I felt there were other poor devils still in, so lent my very little strength to haul them in. I set to work patching up those who had sustained burns and minor injuries. The skipper could not have been more helpful. He had hot sweet tea made, cigarettes and the dressings for the burns.

I soon found, whilst running my personal M.I. room that I was more played out than I had at first thought and was forced to rest. We had twenty-three in the boat, all Other Ranks, which is Army jargon for those who are not Commissioned, Warrant, or Non-commissioned Officers. I sat in the sun trying to get warm and stop shivering, when the skipper leaned over his bridge and asked me if I would like a bath. Wet as I had been and still was, there was nothing I wanted more. So first putting my photos and the other things of sentimental value which had been in the anti-gas wallet and had got damp, out to dry in the sun, I climbed the companion and showered. I felt twice the individual afterwards, collected my drying articles and sat again in the sun. Once again the skipper called me and this time invited Jack and myself on to the bridge where we watched the approach of Singapore. More cigarettes were forthcoming and marvel of marvels a glass of beer!

We learned that we were on 'H.M. Sin Aik Lee', a Gunboat and minesweeper, and that the bombing had occurred fifteen miles out of port. We learned about the defences of the island we were approaching, the Japanese air raids and that we were the reinforcements so often talked about in Parliament at home. We docked in Singapore and were distributed by lorries to various assembly grounds, making the journey in two stages and eventually arriving at Haig Road reinforcement lines.

We were given something to eat and spent our time congratulating each other on our escape and looking for missing faces. It was not for three days that we were once again all together and the total loss for the Field Ambulance was apparently one man only. We were very fortunate.

5 *Into Action*

The endless train ride

THAT train journey seemed to go on and on. A few days and nights are months long when there is no comfort, and at best poor light, and not much to see except suffering humanity.

It seemed to get better — or rather to be slightly less bad as time went on. We had had enough trouble for one lifetime with the Japanese when we were in the encampment at Changi. Now we were supposed to be on our way to better conditions — but we were doubtful and not a little cynical.

We stopped once in the early morning and found ourselves on a dead-end siding with no sign of habitation or railway station. Being coupled to the rear of the train was a true 'passion wagon'. From it had spilled a number of chattering females — at that distance it was difficult to say of what nationality, but there for one purpose (or rather, many ends) as the queue of Japanese and Korean guards which passed at an unbelievable speed into and then a little later out of the wagon demonstrated. The whole proceeding could only be of academic interest to most of us, three quarters starved, by disease emaciated, and conscious of manhood only in a curiously detached sort of way.

Soon we were herded back into the truck. We had established some sort of contact with the engine driver and learned from him that we were on our way to Bangkok.

Bangkok evoked imaginations of romantic far eastern capitals — but then so had Singapore — and the ten days between landing and capitulation by the authorities had been too shell-torn and blood-covered to make much of Singapore . . .

* * * * *

The next few days were spent in a frantic attempt to re-equip the unit with all the essentials of clothing and the like. A small amount of medical stores were obtained and an M.I. Room established.

The houses in which were billetted the officers and men, were part of a housing estate — apparently for native Malayans. They had been bombed once or twice and all the civil population had evacuated. There was a considerable amount of the furniture and furnishings left.

I shall never forget the first night I spent there. I had one blanket and a groundsheet between myself and the concrete floor. I tossed and turned and was extremely glad when the usual five a.m. air raid occurred and forced us into the slit trenches. There appeared to be very little opposition to air raids; anti-aircraft defences were plentiful but the four or five fighter aircraft on the island seldom went up until after the bombers had passed; always in formation, and usually twenty-seven in number. I did once see our nearest gun (we called him 'Hair-Trigger Dan') split up a formation by some extremely well placed shells. Most of the time however, they flew over to Singapore extremely high and almost out of range.

On Sunday night, the 8th of the month, there was a bombardment as heavy as some of the London barrages during the 'blitz', and it was awe-inspiring to hear the deep-throated roar of the nearer artillery followed by the 'swoosh!' as the shell travelled on its way.

We received a rude shock the following morning when the local paper announced the fact that the Japanese had made a landing on the island but had been 'contained'. This sounded like the usual polite fiction to which we had become accustomed so it was not surprising when our own R.A.S.C. who were for the time being unemployed went up to the front as infantry. We were all very confident however, and anxious in spite of our personal deficiencies to get into action. We had been supplied with an almost complete set of medical equipment and it was not long before we sent out a Dressing Station to the front line.

The bombers became more frequent now and we more careless of them. We heard that they were diving, both bombing and machine gunning at the front and wondered how many of our aircraft were up there too. In point of fact there were not any, and indeed on Tuesday, 10th February, the five remaining planes on the island left for safer climes!

Wednesday, 11th February, was I believe, the first day for us to move. We took over some private houses a few hundred yards away as a Main Dressing Station. This was in the Galang Palang Road, opposite the Yock Eng School. At the Dressing Station there were Red Crosses everywhere, one of them being spread out for the benefit of airmen. It was here that I first saw the futility of our struggle. We had heard tremendous rumours about the sky being darkened by Allied 'planes and of Aircraft carriers in the bay, but we knew that there would be no evacuation; that if things came to a bad enough pass we should have to fight to a finish or capitulate. We plumped, outwardly for the former, but we knew (or felt that we knew) that it would be the latter. The battle was not yet lost however, and casualties began pouring into the Dressing Station.

Some men came back dead, some died on our hands and a few were sent to the re-inforcement camp. Here we suffered our next loss. One of the ambulance drivers who was late in taking shelter in a ditch from a coming shell, was killed.

After a few days on Saturday 14th February, we moved into the Municipal Buildings in Singapore town. It was a grand, well-built place and very satisfactory for the purpose for which we required it. We set up a more efficient operating theatre and a larger hospital. Casualties began to increase and together with the civilian refugees the place was most of the time in a turmoil. There were cases of cowardice (none of us felt brave) and of avoidance of work, but taken by and large the Field Ambulance showed up well. The M.Os did particularly good operative work and particularly a young Chinese lady doctor, Mary Tan, who was cool and calm throughout. Once or twice the shells landed unpleasantly close and the bombs were not far away, but we were not hit.

There were some quite interesting experiences there; for example the electricity supply was obviously very erratic and unreliable by that time. It was part of my job to supervise the movement of patients and ensure the smooth flow of casualties from their admission into the hospital to the operating theatres which were in the basement. Sometimes we found that the lights had just failed in the middle of an operation, and so I organised a corps of men, the 'sick, lame and lazy' as we used to call them — the walking wounded, holding candles in their hands ready to light them the moment the electricity went out and then to march into the operating theatre not the least bit sterile and to stand round whilst the surgeon continued his operation by candlelight.

On the infamous Sunday, 15th February, 1942, in the morning, I went for the rations. I had not been out of the Municipal Buildings since we had moved in and the sight that met my eyes was a revelation. Everywhere there was desolation and destruction. Over-turned flaming cars, demolished houses, trailing wires, heaps of wreckage where there had been multiple collisions. We went through it all at a lively pace and I was not sorry when, negotiating a pile of debris consisting of an ambulance upside down, a burnt out civilian car, and an army lorry which had crashed into the two, we turned into the sport's ground where the ration dump was. They were bombing and shelling very near that afternoon and collecting rations was a business of grabbing a crate of rations and squatting behind a stack of them for protection. While we were there, an N.C.O. appeared wearing a soft field service cap. We looked at him in amazement and he told us that really of course the war was over, Division had capitulated at four o'clock and we were wasting our time. However, we loaded up and started on our journey back to the unit. All the way back we were continually stopped and asked if there was any truth in the rumour. We said. "No!" but when we turned into the Municipal Buildings however, I found it was true — the O.C. said so.

That afternoon I finished a bottle I had managed to win and everybody seemed to make a descent on the stores. In the midst of it all the C.O. sent for me to tell me that I was to relieve three or four people on their job for that night, which often seemed to happen to me!

The next morning I went to bed. I had worked eight days during which I had had only a total of eight hours sleep in cat naps, because we had been so very busy. I was not going to be wanted for a little while so I put somebody else on to look after any casualties coming in and wrapped myself in a blanket and lay down on the concrete floor of the Municipal Building and went to sleep. I slept I believe, for fourteen hours.

So far, the reader could be forgiven if he or she thought that it wasn't such a bad War after all. As a young man the challenge had appealed, and the rapidly changing scene inevitable in a busy Service life helped to create the illusion of one big holiday from normal life and work. But the reality had always been there; the knowledge that family and friends were in constant danger from bombs; that it was not impossible that our country could be invaded; that all the training and preparation must end (if there was any meaning to it) in seeing bloody action.

I wrote a lot of the foregoing at a time when it was not possible to put feeling into words, for fear of the feelings taking charge; and because the words could and undoubtedly would be read by friends and possibly foes. Now the reality had come home. Two years of hard work, a voyage almost round the world, bombed at sea, drifting in the water, landed like a drowned rat, hard casualty work under fire, and now this final indignity — of being surrendered to the enemy.

That was what hit me, and perhaps hurt me most then — that a General somewhere, no doubt rightly, had surrendered 'Fortress Singapore' and me with it. I had not raised my hands unable to continue to face danger. We, certainly I, felt betrayed.

What had gone wrong? This enormous volume of stores, these multitudes of men, ships, it seemed, for the asking, and facing (we were told) an ill-equipped illiterate untrained mob with no modern weapons? Prisoners-of-War — and for how long? Suddenly the young man who joined the Territorial Army had disappeared. Maturity had fallen like a mantle around me.

Fatalistically I decided there was nothing I could do — so I went to sleep.

6 *Captivity — Bamboo and barbed wire*

Last train journey

IT HAD been my turn to sit close to the gap in the door and as daylight came in, suddenly as it always did, I found the train was crossing a river, a wide river with many sampans used as houseboats and other craft and a most characteristic smell. I thought we were passing through Bangkok — maybe we were — but in any event not long afterwards the train came to its final halt. It was very hot. We were ordered out, lined up, counted, again and again, until they got the figures to their satisfaction.

We unloaded the goods wagons which contained our kitbags or boxes. There were only a few handcarts. I carried one end of a box with rope handles with other things piled on it. My small kit was on my back.

How far it is from Bampong to Non-Pladuk the geographer can say — it seemed interminable — fiendishly hot, dirty and dusty and exhausting to muscles cramped up for five days. Searched by the Japanese crudely and cruelly; kit and personal belongings stolen; sold some quickly to prevent it being stolen, and to get Thai dollars. A meal, of God knows what; drop exhausted on to a bamboo staging with a precious thin blanket wrapped round and all one's worldly goods clutched under the head as a pillow. To fall asleep — a deep sleep of exhaustion — and perhaps in dreams to recall that other march from Singapore town into captivity . . .

* * * * *

EXTRACT FROM THE SECRET SESSION SPEECHES OF MR. CHURCHILL

> 'On the night of February 8th 1942 about 5,000 Japanese made a lodgment on the north-western corner of the island . . . After five or six days . . . the army and fortress surrendered . . . The lack of any effective counterattack by the 18th Division which arrived in such high spirits and good order, and never seem to have had their chance, is criticised'.

Two days later the first Japanese to enter the building drew up at the door. He greeted the local bigwigs like long lost friends and naturally every facility was given to him. He carried proudly the sword of his fathers. He stood five feet nothing!

From then the usual (or what I suppose is usual) scenes took place in Singapore. A few of the worst offenders against Nipponese might were killed, civilians were interned, friendly enemies put to work and groups of men marched off to Changi barracks for imprisonment.

It was not long however, before we were forced to move away from the sea front, with its now silent battery of Bofors and howitzers, to a deserted girls' school in Sofia Road, near to Government House.

Here were established already the 196 Field Ambulance, and with them we cleared up and discharged the lightly wounded cases in our care. From there we daily watched the emblem of the rising sun floating in the breeze from the big buildings and saw the 'planes no longer fighting, dipping and wheeling in the clear air. Our rations here began to suffer too. There began to be a larger portion of rice and a lot less of the other constituents. We found evidence that there were more people on the island knowing more than was good for them in a diary left by a careless girl who had had a holiday not long before in the state of Johore.

The Japanese seemed to spend most of their time hauling all the artillery in the neighbourhood into the grounds of Government House, or else in fraternising with our troops. On the 25th of the month I was sent in charge of an advance party to Changi, where most of the Division already was. We marched there from Singapore Town, the distance being something like seventeen miles. It was hot.

The native Malays and Chinese were helpful to us. Surreptitiously, when the Japanese guards were not looking, they would give us tea and gula malacca which is a kind of sugary substance and little sweet cakes made of coconut; but they were very respectful to the Japanese. They adopted the view that they were conquered, that they were occupied and that co-operation with the occupying forces was the sensible thing.

We were at Changi for two days only when the unit marched in; an hour later however we were told that we were not to stay and were transported to Loyang village, a village close to the Boom Fort near Changi point.

We stayed at Loyang for just over a week. Moves seemed to be part of our lives, although apart from that inconvenience and the steadily rising proportion of rice in the diet, our treatment by the Japs gave no other cause for complaint at that time.

Whilst here we ran yet another hospital and I conducted shorthand classes in the evenings. I also began carving a set of chess men in the true tradition of all prisoners-of-war.

I next fell sick. A fever, which it must be admitted puzzled the M.Os, took me in its grip and I was evacuated with the remainder of the patients to Roberts Hospital at Changi. This happened one day before the unit moved up into the same area.

A day or so after I had moved in, and by surreptitious glances at my own thermometer had decided that my temperature was once again normal, the Quartermaster came to see me in hospital and asked me if I would like a job and apparently could have it if I could get out of bed in time. That same day I coerced the M.O. to let me get out, in spite of a very groggy 'Singapore foot'. This was a type of foot rot which is messy and painful and is known the world over to the Forces of the Crown and is usually given the name most applicable to the area in which it is contracted. It normally is cured by air and sun, and sometimes liberal dosing with spirit (extremely painful) and talcum powder — or at least it was then.

The job I was to do was Q.M.S. for the Dysentery Wing — a wing of the hospital to be commanded by the O.C. 198 Field Ambulance, with an 'A' staff of that unit, 'Q' staff of 197 and ward staff of all three. In spite of a minus quantity of equipment, and a much reduced amount of drugs we started up. So there I was in the Dysentery Wing, and likely to stay for a while. Life was not too unpleasant however, time passed very quickly because I had a job to do. The deadly enemy was boredom.

I had a diary covering the events up to capitulation but tore it up on that memorable 15th February. I wrote in a kind of booklet I made up in the Camp:

'What a strange admixture of weather this is. Day after day both sun and rain, calm and wind, heat and cold; very little seasonal weather; no dusk or gloaming. I have known in one day the sun, which here is almost always nearly overhead, to be so hot as to require only a modicum if any of clothes and grateful shade is eagerly sought. The day seems to hold its breath and no leaf stirs on the banana trees or coconut palms; the sky is overcast and the cacophony of insect and bird sounds, ceases. Then there is a rustling, a whispering and a murmuring in the foliage; the leaves stir, and the clouds scud before an ever-increasing breeze; increasing and increasing until the dust and leaves rise and scurry before it and pieces of paper are tossed and tormented in the eddies. Then one or two spots of rain appear assuming in the dust the size of a florin and pitter-patter on thatched roof and concrete building in a very tornado, down comes the rain — a solid scintillating slashing deluge. Nothing can withstand its vigour; the very trees bow before its might while the shrubs make humble obeisance with their heads touching the ground. Streams and rivulets appear where there was arid earth — the gullies overflow — even the flies take shelter.

Then gradually it abates and the sun which has for a little while been hiding his face comes and shines again as though he ought to turn the bedraggled world into a steaming mass again. Our reveille is officially half past seven, because under the new Japanese dispensation of time that is the first ray of daylight. I always have time before breakfast to shave and having tidied up the last night's debris to read for a few minutes before the meal. At about ten, i.e. half an hour after the meal, I go to the office and spend the morning in performing the tasks of my office as Q.M.S. They are not onerous here because we have so little stores to deal with, but they are irksome for that same reason, and compromise is the order of the day.

Lunch, or as it is known, tiffin, follows at about one o'clock and back again at two. There is usually very little to do in the afternoon beyond a certain amount of clerical work on the rationing side. This done I fill in the afternoon with miscellaneous typing or writing and similar jobs.

After dinner, which we have at about six, a wash, and for the sake of old times a change of clothes is indicated and a read and smoke if we are fortunate on the porch.

There follows supper at about eight o'clock and the night is upon us. Evenings are spent fairly evenly distributed between playing bridge, a half dozen of us singing old songs in harmony for self-amusement, or merely letting the conversation wander. On Saturday evenings there is usually an organised sing-song with musical accompaniment under the aegis of one of the three Field Ambulances; on Mondays a concert organised by the Australian Red Cross. Sometimes I walk; partly for the exercise itself and partly because I feel it good to get away from the crowd, if only for a short time; the company of the same people continuously is apt to be palling!

Fortunately we still have plenty to read, by dint of swapping, and the weekly ration of cigarettes though meagre does at least make life bearable for a few days.'

I have always liked writing and once the initial shock of the fact of becoming a prisoner had begun to be accepted I found I had a burning desire to put things down on paper. By and large this meant giving up something else in order to have the paper. A lot of what I used for typing on was Army Form OO (or toilet paper). Typewriters were no problem since they were plentiful and not many were in use. Also from something I had learned as a boy I was able to 'bind' the sheets into some form of books, covered in cardboard from food cartons. I have these booklets still, with the imprint of the bottoms of tins in the card, stained with the rains of Siam — the typing fading.

The book from which the above extracts come was called (incorrectly)

'Five Continents' but it was read by others, which is all any author can ask.

Drawings made in coloured pencil by the Author in the early days of captivity

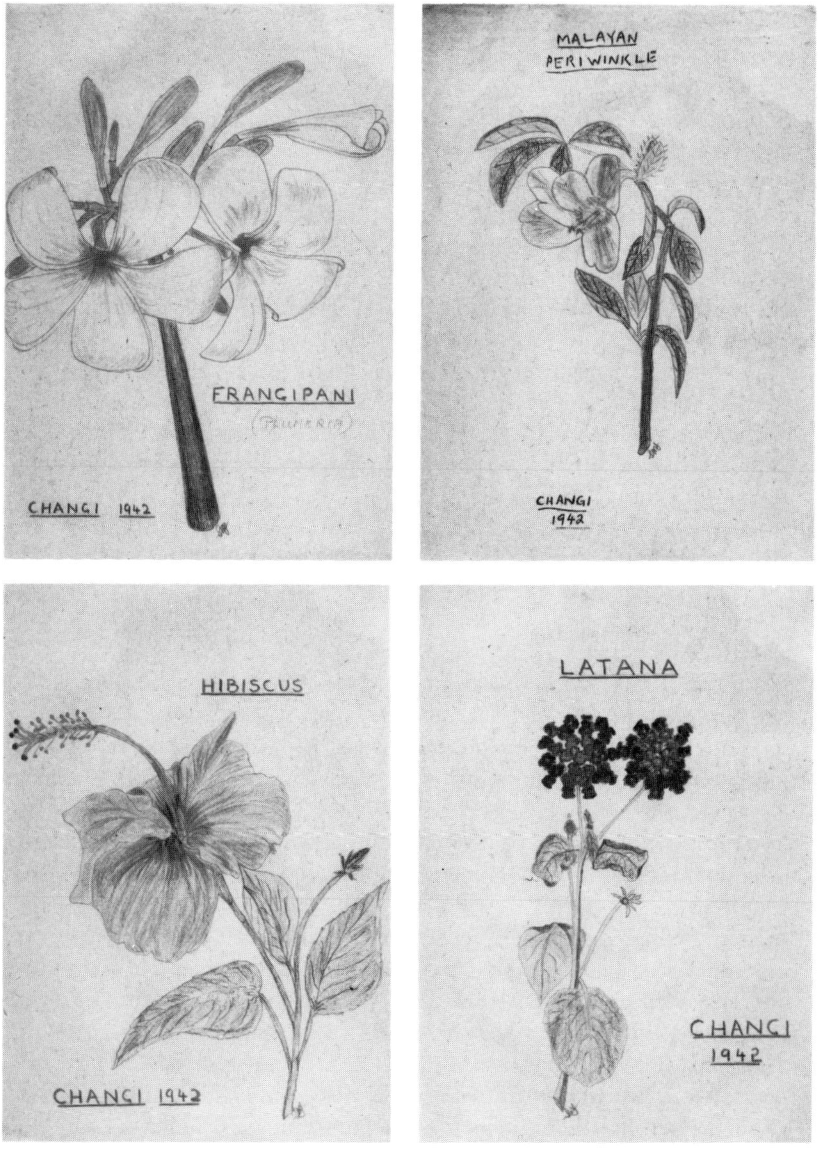

7 *The First Year 1942/43*

The Sleep March

IT WAS weird to start marching just before nightfall and to find suddenly that the light had gone, but we tramped on. It was the stuff that dreams, or perhaps nightmares, are made of.

Soon many found that they had over-estimated their own resilience and determination, and the partially metalled road became strewn with articles which the owners had decided represented more weight to carry than they were worth to keep.

Some clothes, even a blanket or two, tins, boxes, books, all, left to the elements on a road on the edge of the jungle, as the march dragged on. Not a march really — more a wild staggering of exhausted men lurching from one uneven step to the next, turning ankles in potholes, gaining blisters, longing for the sleep which should have covered this night, and wishing advantage had been taken during the day before. But 'they' had not told us we were to march that night, on practically empty stomachs, emaciated and ill. Friends linked arms to stop staggering or worse falling down.

It was even possible, however improbable it sounds, to fall into a half sleep, and fantasise on the first year in Singapore . . .

* * * * *

I said in an interview held recently at the Imperial War Museum:

> 'Life was full of change however. For a period I was what was called a Ward Master, which is the equivalent of a Hospital Sister, doing precisely that kind of work. Another time I was in the stores, foraging, scrounging, experimenting, particularly experimenting — for example we found that banana skins would ferment and make a form of alcohol, part of which was drunk, and part of which was used as an antiseptic wash.
>
> On another occasion I became Entertainments Officer. We were moved about from job to job partly by choice. If one got tired of a job, one said so and somebody else was only too pleased to take it on, but it was a very static period. It was rather like the phoney war in Britain during the war, nothing much was happening.
>
> We were just prisoners, with our food supply rapidly diminishing, (because we had European food stocks with us which we rationed,

which in the nature of things gradually disappeared) and more and more replaced by the plain boiled white rice which was the staple diet. Also with the medical supplies, the same thing happened. I remember having a dispensary for medical supplies and on one occasion counting the number of bottles that we had, individual single bottles. One would expect to find in a modern hospital perhaps two thousand different bottles and ours I think did not reach one hundred, we were so short of supplies.

We also discovered that we could use latex from rubber trees to stick bandages on to limbs; the bandages normally being white linen supplied from the clothes of the troops; because although we started with reasonable uniforms, we finished, almost all of us, in rags. If you were luxurious you had a tattered shirt and a tattered pair of shorts and a pair of wooden shoes; we called them 'geta', a kind of platform of wood with a strap over the instep. But for most of us it was dressing up in the evening in some form of uniform and during the day simply wearing a G string.'

The little booklet already referred to finishes:

'Our diet since the capitulation has deteriorated considerably. This is not surprising — it is only necessary to keep us alive.

The personnel operating the Dysentery Wing have the following dietary:

For breakfast, rice boiled and usually unsweetened. On good mornings a porridge consisting of 20% wheat and the remainder ground rice. Tea, made from the local brand, which is a bastard china, without sugar or milk.

At Tiffin precisely the same sometimes embellished by a fried rice roll. The fat is good for one but it tastes horribly rancid and the same sort of tea!

For dinner we spread ourselves. A thick gravy made up of minute quantities of beans and meat with plain rice, or on halcyon days a meat pasty or roll, followed by sweet rice or again a rice flour pasty or roll. No tea!

For supper again just plain rice and plain tea. As will be seen this leaves much to be desired and there is some vitamin deficiency. A and D are obtained periodically in milk on rice, B1 in ground nut meal made into rissoles, B1 and B2 in yeast home-grown and drunk in 1 oz doses. C sometimes in the occasional green vegetables such as egg-fruit and papaya.'

I decided to start a diary on May 20th 1942 nearly three months after becoming a prisoner in a camp in Singapore. My first entry recorded how very cold I felt, although the temperature was 77 degrees. We observed Empire Day and started to hold concerts with me wishing that I had not lost my band and its instruments at the bottom of the ocean. It was possible to get very bored, but the more sensible among us found plenty of activity, physical and mental, in order to prevent this happening.

It was about this time during June that I among many others started to contract illnesses which remained with us on and off for the whole of the period of our prisoner-of-war days. I recorded a violent attack of diaorrhea pushing the score up to fourteen and we began to get sores particularly in infections of the feet, and around the scrotum.

We were allowed to despatch our first POW card home but did not really expect either for it to go or for us to receive any in return. By June 21st of that year the number of deaths in the wing from dysentery or allied causes had reached one hundred; in fact the deaths from disease in the whole hospital area were greater than the deaths resulting from wounds. On July 20th all ranks over Lieutenant Colonel plus four hundred troops and some Red Cross personnel started off on a journey to Japan, although in the meantime there had been two or three small expeditions 'up country' but we did not know where.

P.O.W. CEMETERY

A row of sombre crosses and a grave,
Whose yawning mouth its prey has just received:
There, six feet down, a blanket for a shroud,
An outstretched form that once was virile man;
The Union Jack in unattended folds,
Beside a stretcher stained with mud and gore;
The cynical hypocrisy of those
Who made this service necessary now:
And threading all, in tones monotonous,
The words of him who earnestly would seek
To launch the erring spirit on its path
To the Empyrean or its counterpart.
You whispering trees observe that here and now
The reckoning day will come — we sternly vow.

26.4.42

DYSENTERY

O! Little germ,
You worm!
You swinish little beast!
Amoeba or bacillus,
Why do you have to feast
On decent healthy virile man?

You little newt!
You brute!
O! Stinking little pest;
Obnoxious and infective
You're at your smelly best
As parasite to mighty man.

May you die
Of starvation,
When you try
Recreation
On the inside of a self-respecting man!

Nuisance;
Scram!!
29.4.42

Life in the prison camp was also improved by the setting up of a first class concert party, with, as was inevitable, the female impersonators, who it must be admitted, did their jobs extremely well and were thoroughly convincing. The diary says:

May 20th, 1942 *"Felt very cold when we got up this morning, found a stiff cool breeze, felt like putting a shirt on but found temperature was 77°F. Decided to be hardy and left shirt off."*

May 24th *"Today is Empire Day! Had a good sing-song last night, two men taking off the Weston Brothers extremely well. Cigarette rations are issued on a Friday. I find I usually have none of my original issue by Saturday. Fortunately there are other ways."*

May 27th *"Went over to see Sgt. Egleton in hospital tonight. He may have dengue. I am doing his job. On the way back noticed a crowd around a Jap who had apparently brought in two cases, accidents, I suppose. I wish they had been bomb wounds — our bombs! Went last night to a Red Cross concert — very good,* *extremely good sketch about fertility and propagation. Wish I had the RamSacs (my dance band) here."*

June 6th *"I seem to have neglected this book. Went to 18 Div. concert party last night jolly good show; some of the same artists as we had in Scotland at Lauder. I've got a foul cold and not even the advantage of cool air to clear the head. Blast this place!"*

June 7th *"I slept extremely well last night which is unusual as I am sleeping badly nowadays."*

June 9th *"I am sleeping better although my trouble which first made its appearance at Sofia Road* [*tinia pedis — foot rot*] *has recurred. It is progressing satisfactorily. Some very heavy bombers left here this morning, Whither?"*

June 10th *"Still feeling groggy. Spent some time at a spelling bee."*

June 11th *"I find I have conquered a fear I used to have of the dead. At one time I remember I hated the idea of seeing a dead person or of sleeping near one. I have seen so many corpses most of them extremely unpleasant and I no longer feel revulsion and as I went to sleep a curious thought struck me that I could quite coolly sleep if one of my companions had just died."*

June 12th *"Last night a local portable gramophone played some sentimental tunes reviving memories. It is pleasant while it lasts but it brings in train an overwhelming nostalgia."*

June 13th *"Had a violent attack of acute diarrhoea yesterday pushing the score up to fourteen. The combination of climate, strange food, and lack of exercise make these attacks frequent and terrifying; feel better today. Oh to be in a cool climate with reasonable European food."*

June 15th *"It is time that I recorded my appreciation of the devotion shown me by my batman. He has served me faithfully on his own accord for the seventeen weeks which have elapsed since capitulation and without pay. Now that we have been paid a modicum for our services during May by the Japs, he will only accept a nominal amount. It is very gratifying but embarrassing."*

June 18th *"Yesterday a party of 53 ORs (Other Ranks) was called to go with the working parties up the mainland. It included two WOs and I felt rocky. It was decided however to send only one and a Staff Sergeant so I breathe again. My intestines are very bad so I went to bed much depressed. Had a good night however."*

June 20th *"Despatched our first POW card home today, one's own message but we were advised it should be short and preferably in block letters. I wonder if the other way is working too."*

June 21st *"The number of deaths in this wing from dysentery or allied causes reached one hundred yesterday. The deaths from disease in the whole hospital area are greater than deaths from wounds. This does not take into account the deaths prior to the establishment of the hospital."*

June 25th *"The Japanese have a 'scheme'* [*military manoeuvres*] *on and we have total blackout every evening now. This we understand is for seventeen days. I wonder it it's because of the presence of allied planes."*

June 26th *"A party went up to the mainland today — some of our units were involved. I wonder if we shall all be split up."*

June 27th *"Had a foretaste of civilisation last night. Part of the canteen stocks* [*from the Nips of course*] *was chocolate. I bought a few and with my weekly ration of cigarettes contrived to smoke and eat chocolate at the same time — a very civilised sensuality. To cap it there was a celebrity concert of better class music and songs thoroughly enjoyable. The black-out continues."*

June 29th *"Jack Sugg* [*my R.A.S.C. Sergeant Major friend*] *came over to see us yesterday, no news of any importance. I must go out to see him some afternoon in the near future. We have a copy of the Syonan* [*Singapore*] *Times but it is merely the usual splurge in propaganda. There is Cholera in Singapore. I am having an injection today."*

July 1st *"There is much activity now. Planes went out before it was light this morning and there was an hour of continual explosions from what it is difficult to say. I have heard the theory of depth charges. We have an astounding rumour of Churchill's speech. Hope it's correct."*

July 2nd *"Went out to visit Jack Sugg yesterday. He told us their Captain had been beaten up by the Japs down in Singapore."*

July 10th *"Japanese time is one and a half hours ahead of (British) Singapore time, so our Sunrise is now always about quarter to eight and sunset at eight. There is much air activity but I think it is propaganda only. Our diet does not improve and our cigarette ration is down."*

July 12th *"We have been looking forward to signs of action because of the good news or rumours we have been having but nothing seems to happen. It is very disappointing. I have started German classes."*

July 17th *"I went last night to see the concert 'New Pins and Needles' in the Southern Area Camp. A Bombadier took the part of Gloria d'Earie. He kept a straight face and played only serious parts including the dance and would have convinced anyone who unlike ourselves did not know it was a man but a woman. Shades of the Holborn Empire. I dreamed last night I was with two or three women but was impotent — Oh for vitamin E."*

July 20th *"Last night we said goodbye to our ADMS. He has to go with the remainder of those over the rank of Lieutenant Colonel to Japan. With them are going about four thousand troops and some Red Cross personnel. We are losing Staff/Sergeant Dunlop."*

July 22nd *"Had another goodbye last night 'Camp Pie' the hospital magazine organised a concert. Bobby Spong, comedienne impersonator was there, very good indeed. I said my personal goodbye to Joe Biggs, my drummer in the band, who is going with this party."*

July 23rd *"We went to see 'Dover Road', the play by A.A. Milne performed by members of the 18th Div. in their area. Good stage arrangements, splendid scenery, good orchestra under Dennis East, the violinist, good characterisation. Parts of Ann and Eustasia both well taken. The Japanese expedition is temporarily cancelled. Lost control of the sea? Very bad night — too much perspiration."*

July 30th *"Had a concert in this area last night at which Gloria d'Earie appeared. Her (or rather his) name is Arthur Butler mimicked Gracie Fields, Carmen Miranda, Phyllis Robbins and others, all extremely good."*

August 3rd *"Bank Holiday Monday. I wonder what they will be doing at home today. Two years and eleven months of War — keeps going! Went into the Steward's Store today — amazing variety of food, carrots from Australia, carrots from Malaya, asparagus from Tokyo, asparagus from California, green peas from Singapore, mango chutney from Calcutta, Ostomalt from Hayes, table jellies from Cape Town, margarine from Manilla, radio malt from BDH London, Heinz soup from Leamington, Canada, Cow & Gate glucose from Guildford, bread from Changi bakeries.* [*We soldiers saw very little of this in the days to come.*]*"*

August 11th *"Saw Gloria d'Earie again last night at a concert in the old cinema. That young man Arthur Butler is amazing. The apparent sight of a woman on the stage gives one an immense fillip. It makes life worth living for a little while longer; these concert party people are doing a great work — our morale is extremely high."*

August 14th *"Last night the electric current came on again in some of the blocks*

— it was a real pleasure to see the lights after being used to the dim glow of hurricane lamps."

August 15th [**1942**] *"Six months ago today we capitulated. Yesterday we heard that a boat from Hong Kong is here with the women and children from there to collect those here for repatriation. There has been a dearth of news. Slept extremely badly because I was thinking about the novel I am writing. I am half way through it. Yesterday we had an arts and craft exhibition — I won a first class mention with my booklet 'Five Continents'. We hear that it has been announced in England that pay has increased, I believe mine is by 1s. 6d. per day equals 10s. 6d. per week. I shall count this in my credits henceforth."*

August 17th *"We had our own lights on last night — and the punkah — it was grand to read comfortably and not have to use the hurricane lamp. The first Jap party has gone and there is a rumour of a Red Cross ship in Singapore. A further rumour states that it has letters and parcels on board for us. We held a German conversation because the official classes have stopped."*

August 22nd *"A Red Cross ship has arrived in Singapore, we think it is Portugese. It appears to come from South Africa and we have had from it Vitamin A and C sweets. Jam and soup. Also maize meal. Somebody must have used some good foresight. The main thing about the tropics is the number of insects and small animal life; barking lizards, croaking bull frogs and red ants, giant ants, black ants, flying ants, spiders of all sorts, dragonflies measuring four inches across the wings, wasps, hornets, blue insects (I don't know the name of) and of course the cockroach. The mosquitoes, some harmless some malaria carrying and big black and white ones, dengue; and nowadays everyone, everyone, has bugs. I get about two a week. I am very lucky. Sometimes snakes."*

August 26th *"I have just finished writing a novel. It needs typing of course. I feel a certain amount of satisfaction. It is entitled 'Some Blunt Instrument' by Ernest Wood."*

August 31st *"The Japanese have ordered that we should sign a 'parole' form stating 'I solemnly swear upon my honour that I will not attempt to escape.' The whole camp (60,000) with only one or two exceptions have refused to sign it! Tomorrow we are to have an IJA roll call. (Tenko)."*

September 1st *"We had our roll call and it is apparent some of the Japanese soldiers are absolutely . . . [There is a gap here because parts of the diary were cut out physically, later] stood about in the sun all morning. This afternoon I played football for the first time for eleven years. I played as goal keeper. Felt very strange. Three years ago today was general mobilisation."*

September 2nd *"The reprisals promised if we refused to sign, started today. The whole of 18th Div. and possibly some other areas were moved suddenly into real concentration at Selarang. 1,500 men and officers to a block meant to hold two hundred in eight blocks. The hospital was told to move but we put up a squeal and stuck tight. We are at present two sealed camps incapable of communication or even getting our rations. Colonel Craven came to talk to us to warn us against a futile attempt to escape and to tell us what happened to an officer and three men who were caught. The four were made to sit and watch preparations for their execution throughout an hour. Then the four were put against a wall and four riflemen (Sikhs) took up their positions. Twenty rounds were needed to kill them off! There is no compassion . . .* [*Gap*]"

September 3rd *"Three years from outbreak of war, 11 a.m. and a Sunday. Today is Thursday."*

September 5th *"Late last night we were ordered to sign the form. Today the others started coming back from Selarang. It was pleasant to see them. Their spirit apparently was good, they improvised concerts and sang 'God Save the King' and 'Land of Hope and Glory', a fine gesture. Three men were wounded due to infringement of restrictions."*

Japanese propaganda paper for Singapore

24 RAIDERS BLASTED

Fukuoka, Aug. 9—(Domei)—Nippon interceptors and anti-aircraft batteries are known by 3 p.m. Wednesday to have shot down at least 12 enemy planes and seriously crippled a dozen others in the course of interception operations yesterday when enemy aircraft attacked northern Kyushu. Preliminary reports indicate that damage caused to our side was slight.

The Syonan Shimbun

Editorial Office: 403, Upper Serangoon Road. Telephone: 5446-7

Subscription Office: 401, Upper Serangoon Road. Telephone: 6361

No. 842 — FRIDAY, AUG. 10, 2605 — PRICE $10 MONTHLY

NEW TUG-BOATS

Alor Star, Aug. 8—(Domei)—A certain shipbuilding yard in Northern Malai has launched five large-size towing craft, which when fitted out with diesel motors, will be capable of pulling three or four 100-ton vessels at the speed of six to seven knots, it was learned to-day. These new type tug-boats are expected to bolster greatly Malai coastwise shipping.

Enemy Air Bases, War Vessels In Okinawa Waters Blasted

Tokyo, Aug. 9. (Domei)—The Nippon air force carried out a successful night attack on the Okinawa sector last night.

According to a dispatch reaching here from a Nippon base in the South-western Islands this morning, our airmen struck at enemy airfields on Main Okinawa Island and also surface craft in adjacent waters during Wednesday night.

Returning crew members of our air force reported that a big fire was caused to start in the target area on Iyejima Island, northwest of Main Okinawa Island, while Naka airfields on Okinawa were also set ablaze at a point.

Striking at enemy surface vessels our air force sank one enemy warcraft and damaged another, both of unidentified category.

EDITORIAL

GIVE GENEROUSLY

NEW IMPERIAL HOUSEHOLD OFFICE CREATED

Tokyo, Aug. 10, (Domei)—A new office of the Household of His Imperial Highness the Crown Prince following the granting of Imperial sanction will be officially established, effective Aug. 10, the Imperial Household Ministry announced.

LORD STEWARD

The Imperial Household Ministry also announced the appointment of Baron Shigeto Hozumi as Lord Steward and concurrently Grand Chamberlain to His Imperial Highness the Crown Prince, who is attending the sixth year course of the Elementary Department of the Peers School in the best of health.

Baron Shigeto Hozumi, who has been graciously granted the Government Service rank of Shinninkan, hails from Tokyo. An authority on Nippon civil

Storming Attacks Take Heavy Toll Of Enemy On Balik Papan Front

A Nippon Base on the Southern Front, Aug. 9. (Domei)—Incessant storming attacks by Nippon forces all along the Balik Papan front have taken a mounting toll of enemy lives after having checked the advance of the enemy. As the result of our organized storming tactics, the enemy forces have already lost 30 per cent. of their total combat personnel since they landed at Balik Papan.

In the course of the past month, enemy forces have only been able to occupy a part of Balik Papan City and Manggar and Soepingan airfields. Worried over the failure of their operations, enemy forces recently attempted to advance along the Samarinda Road. However, upon meeting our ironwall defence lines, they have been stopped.

Meanwhile, our daring storming parties are continuing their intrepid assaults

NIPPON ONLY NATION THAT STILL UPHOLDS INTERNATIONAL MORALITY

Cambodian Foreign Minister's Striking Tribute

Tokyo, Aug. 9, (Domei)—"Nippon is the only nation left in the world whose profession of international morality can be trusted, and Asiatic traditions and Asiatic nations can be truthfully said to be typified and represented by Nippon."

This is the opinion of Son Ngoc Thanh, Foreign Minister of the Cambodian Government, expressed in an article appearing in today's issue of the Nippon Times.

The Cambodian Foreign Minister, paying tribute to Nippon's heroic Special Attack Corps, said the valiant spirit of the Corps "has been nurtured in the blood of the Nippon race for thousands of years." "It is the true expression of the Yamato spirit," he added.

SELF-SACRIFICE

He said this spirit can really be understood by Asiatics only and "it is the highest expression of self-sacrifice." "What profoundly shook the souls of Asiatic youths, causing them to re-

tic youths," he said. He added there is no room for doubt that Cambodian youths will find the same spirit among themselves and fully demonstrate it.

Bitterly criticizing the enemy's methods of warfare, he said: "The barbarous Americans are completely disregarding the rules of international morality, not to mention international law. Brute force which they call justice, dominates the war strategy of the Americans who are aiming solely to advance their own ends. It is a mistake to think that these modern vandals can conquer Nippon.

DESPITE RAIDS

Despite the fact that enemy

Order re signing of illegal parole

COPY.

SELERANG SPECIAL ORDER No.3
dated
4th SEPTEMBER 1942.
-----------:o:-----------

1. On 30th August 1942, I, together with my Area Commanders was summoned to the Conference House, Changi Gaol, where I was informed by the representative of Major General Shimpei Fukuye, G.O.C. Prisoner of War Camps, Malaya, that all Prisoners of War in Changi Camp were to be given forms of promise not to escape, and that all were to be given an opportunity to sign this form.

2. By the Laws and Usages of War a prisoner of war cannot be required by the Power holding him to give his parole, and in our Army those who have become prisoners of war are not permitted to give their parole. I pointed out this position to the Japanese Authorities.

3. I informed the representative of Major General Shimpei Fukuye that I was not prepared to sign the form, and that I did not consider that any Officers or men in the Changi Camp would be prepared to sign the form. In accordance with the orders of the Japanese Authorities, all prisoners of war were given an opportunity to sign. The result of that opportunity is well known.

4. On the 31st August I was informed by the Japanese Authorities that those personnel who refused to sign the certificate would be subjected to "measures of severity", and that a refusal to sign would be regarded as a direct refusal to obey a regulation which the Imperial Japanese Army considered it necessary to enforce.

5. Later, on the night of 31st August/1st September, I was warned that on the 1st September all prisoners of war persisting in refusal to sign were to move by 1800 hrs to Selerang Barrack Square. I confirmed, both on my own behalf and in the name of the prisoners of war, our refusal to sign.

6. The move to Selerang Barrack Square was successfully accomplished on the same afternoon.

7. I and the Area Commanders have been in constant conference with the Imperial Japanese Army and have endeavoured by negotiation to have the form either abolished or at least modified. All that I have been able to obtain is that that which was originally a demand, accompanied by threats of "measures of severity", has now been issued as an official order of the Imperial Japanese Government.

8. During the period of the occupation of the Selerang Barrack S Square the conditions in which we have been placed have been under constant consideration. These may be briefly described as such th existence therein will result in a very few days in the outbreak o epidemic and the most serious consequences to those under my Com and inevitable death to many. Taking into account the low state health in which many of us now are, and the need to preserve our intact as long as possible, and in the full conviction that my actio were the circumstances in which we are now living known to them, wou meet with the approval of His Majesty's Government, I have felt it duty to order all personnel to sign the certificate under the duress imposed by the Imperial Japanese Army.

9. I am fully convinced that His Majesty's Government only expects prisoners of war not to give their parole when such parole is to be given voluntarily. This factor can in no circumstances regarded as applicable to our present condition. The responsibili for this decision rests with me, and with me alone, and I fully ac it in ordering you to sign.

10. I wish to record in this Order my deep appreciation of t excellent spirit and good discipline which all ranks have shewn during this trying period.

I look to all ranks to continue in good heart, disciplin and morale.

Thank you all for your loyalty and co-operation.

(Sgd) E.B.HOLMES.
Colo
Commanding British and Australian

SELERANG,
4th September 1942.

8 The Daily Round for the bamboo medic

Mud and Madness

THE rain did not start at the beginning of the march, but the air was heavy and oppressive. The night insects were merciless both in their noise and their attacks.

When the march for the night ended, exhausted, reeling with fatigue it was necessary first to tend to the feet of others, blisters and bruises and here a strained ankle, there a suspect broken toe. Then to join the end of the queue, mess tin in hand, to receive a ration of soggy plain rice and a brew of so-called green tea. Having swallowed it without ceremony (hunger is a great spur) to drop asleep before lying down, on soggy undergrowth or grass or whatever it was, knowing the night was now short and the day would come when perhaps there might be some rest before being goaded up and on.

Pondering on fifteen months gone by; fifteen almost unbelievable months of captivity, sickness and smells, of beatings and executions, of hunger and thirst, heat and cold, friends and enemies, and a desperate struggle to do normal things and retain some touch with the world of the day before yesterday . . .

* * * * *

September 8th *"My book is published but at the moment being re-read for alterations. The glow has gone. [This means simply that I had finished the typing and binding of the book and had allowed it to be read by others. The 'glow' of achievement had faded.]"*

September 18th *"Yesterday was my birthday. It started badly at about four in the morning, a rat decided to investigate my bed. He eventually got thirsty and was drowned in a tub of sewer water. I awoke at seven o'clock with a heavy head. A lazy morning and in the afternoon I walked with J.T. to Jack Sugg. Early evening I watched the football match. Bought a tin of fruit from the canteen and we had one and a half ounces of brandy from before capitulation. What a celebration. Did not get to sleep until about three o'clock."*

September 22nd *"Pay day. First for three weeks and we hear probably the last. There is a Red Cross ship in with eight hundred tons of stuff. We can find little else about it. I wonder if there are letters. I have a vicious cold and returned* *dengue symptoms. We were inspected by the Nips today. They scrutinised our kits. Before they came rumour had it they were searching for forbidden articles and excesses of kit. When they came round it actually appeared almost a welfare visit. Time will show I suppose."*

October 17th *"I have just recovered from another bout of dengue and now have a stye on my left eye, the first since I was about eleven. There seems to have been a constant stream of ships in bearing Red Cross stores. Our diet has improved a little and we have had some personal issues such as cigarettes and sweet biscuits. No letters yet — we need them. The book has so far been received favourably and now in the Officer's Mess. The second is in course of preparation."*

October 25th *"Events are crowding in on each other. The Japs have started evacuating all the other captured islands. We were talking to a Dutchman yesterday who sixteen days ago was in Timor still in Nip hands but with guerillas active . . . [There is a gap here.] They are moving the Java party up country and at last some from one of our areas. One hundred and fifty medical personnel are to go. No news and no letters. In the hospital we are to have a change of OC — already we have had a change of Chief Wardmaster. Yesterday we had an impromptu cinema show. Very old films and a tiny projector in the open air — Jack Sugg came over. There are apparently attempts on the life of his RSM by their men."*

October 29th *"A year ago today we embarked from Liverpool. One year's overseas service. We have a new OC hospital Lieutenant Colonel Collins. Since receiving Red Cross supplies, the Japs have contrary to International Law cut down our issues of food they are . . . [There is a gap here] but very serious. Many troops are going up country."*

November 2nd *"Today the 198 Field Ambulance moved out en masse for up country. We wonder who will go next."*

November 24th *"Yesterday, I was made Wardmaster of the Officers Dysentery Ward. I mustn't grumble as I was out of work but I was having the first rest since I came here. There has been much change in the hospital. I have forty-seven Officers only four of whom are English, remainder Dutch. This is because in the camp there is only a small number of English and the remainder being Dutch, American, Australian and others."*

November 27th *"Four days of being a Wardmaster and I find it not so unpleasant as at first I thought it would be. I had two deaths in the first two days. These Dutchmen seem to make very little fight of it."*

December 9th *"The north easterly monsoons have started and it rains all the* *time. I have never seen it rain so heavily. In addition the Nips have ordered a blackout. We cannot get our washing dry. There is a rumour of other Red Cross ships. There was an orgy of face slapping by the Japs a few days ago."*

December 16th *"Blue ink is scarce hence the red. We may have to write with synthetic ink. There are many activities to raise money and make toys however poor, for the kiddies in Changi jail. There are over one hundred of them. Today for the first time in three years I did some gardening. There is a plot of land outside my bunk which was planted but became overgrown. I made some improvement this afternoon but weeds grow so thickly and quickly. Tomorrow a new Nip GOC takes over here. When the old one Maj. Gen. Shimpei Fukeye went, he was promoted. He sent for our Lt. Cols. gave instructions how they should dress, told them to parade and ordered them to congratulate him. The new GOC has ordered that his route of entry be lined with cheering British soldiers and more than three parts of the camp will be there."*

December 21st *"I have had another attack of fever similar to three I have already had. The fever; headache, backache etc., lasts for three days only. Temperature usually 100 to 103. A rigor of two hours duration; after a week I feel weak, lethargic and generally out of sorts. I have no appetite. I suppose the next attack will come mid-March. I return to work tomorrow. We are making preparations for Christmas."*

December 27th *"Christmas is over. I am very pleased, Christmas day was uneventful our menu being improved by what we had saved from previous issues of rations. On Christmas Eve I had a patient die in the ward and we heard that one of our Sergeants who is in dock with Carcinoma of the liver and lung is on the D.I. list. He died on Boxing morning and the funeral was therefore yesterday afternoon. A good turnout of the whole unit. I notice that the cemetery is extending itself and they are laying it out like a first class landscape garden cemetery at home. We are callous of course. In the evening we had an entertainment by a pair of Dutchmen. One did some superb card tricks and the other mind reading — and there was no fake. Both of the Dutchmen went away and we decided that he should take some cigarettes that were on the floor by my feet and with them make a letter 'W' on the table. His medium was Chappy the RSM. The Dutchman held his wrist lightly not touching his pulse whilst he pressed a forefinger very hard onto the other's wrist. It took him twenty minutes to locate me, find my cigarettes and take them to the table and form the required letter. He says he can hear us thinking. There is absolutely no collusion."*

January 1st 1943 *"Time marches on. As a New Year gift the Japs who celebrated it gave us each a third tin of pineapple and 1/10 bottle of Shamshi, a rice whisky very raw and very potent. We all got merry and joined the officers who were all* *three parts under at midnight. There was noise for hours. No ill effects next day in spite of the time away from them."*

January 17th *"Each day I find another thing to marvel at. So very few men seem to have any sense of social responsibility or any thought as to whether by doing an action in one particular way they would help or hinder a comrade. So very many are petty, selfish, concerned only that they miss nothing, determined to live now and to anyone else careless and thoughtless of the consequences of their action and noisy."*

February 3rd *"Some time ago I made a shove halfpenny board in the carpenter's shop. It has provided some pleasant half hours. I am writing another novel. The ration for a three day period is now sugar 2 oz. tea ½ oz. and 3 oz. ghi, ½ oz. salt, rice 57 ozs., veg as available 24 oz."*

February 12th *"We had today, after two false alarms, a parade of fifteen thousand POWs on the padang, in practice we believe for a big Jap parade on the 15th the anniversary of capitulation. Today I have taken over the management of the cooked food canteen called the 'Supper Bar'."*

March 1st *"I have very nearly finished my second detective novel. We have made friends with a Dutch teaplanter from Java whose name is Charles Le Clerc. He has an idea for a story about Pithecanthropus Erectus. He will tell me it in his own words (fair English) and I will write the book. He will stand the cost of a private publication if no other publisher will accept it."*

March 9th *"There is talk of letters for us at Changi jail. I finished my second book calling it 'Some Person Unknown'. Still managing the 'Supper Bar' — find it very interesting. Had a merciless chin-wag about school days with Stewart Livesley, Corporal of Intelligence. Brought back many memories."*

March 27th *"I was offered the job of hospital steward a little while ago. A good job but turned it down because it stinks of rackets. On the next day naturally I was put on the wards, Ward P2 dysentery (other ranks) but Major Hutchins says I may expect another change and hints at something better."*

April 9th *"Have been very busy lately. Wards, 'Supper Bar' and producing a show at Kokonut Grove with the co-operation of many of my old confreres."*

April 12th *"Monday, Easter Holiday. Kokonut Grove opened as well as being Producer and Compere I am taking a part. My Ward closed down. Mr. Sinden (my Quartermaster) and the 196 are going on an up country party and has asked me to go with him."*

April 14th *"Wednesday. Concert still on. Decided to close down on Thursday but Div. H.Q. have asked for a show on Friday. Much consternation among the boys of 197 in regard to me going. First injection for Plague."*

April 15th *"Concert went well. Today re-vaccination, hope it doesn't take. Started packing stores for up country. I am the QMS for the hospital."*

April 16th *"Friday. Woke with vicious cold? Vaccine fever."*

April 19th *"Had two more injections Cholera and Plague. My arms are very sore. Have assembled most of the hospital stores but lost my Parker pen in the process. Cold still with me but going I think. Don't know yet when I leave for up country."*

* * * * *

The entry for April 14th reads as though I was a little big-headed about my place in the scheme of things. I had been with the 197 Field Ambulance through many things both in England and here in the prison camp. Moreover the system of discipline and control imposed on us by the Japanese had increased the dependence of the general body of men on their N.C.Os and particularly the senior Warrant Officers.

The Japanese left it to the Lieutenant-Colonel in charge of any unit or group to maintain discipline and even exact punishments if he wished. They did not want to be bothered, especially where large bodies of troops were concerned. The result was that the Lt. Cols. gathered together their junior Officers and their Warrant Officers and N.C.Os — Sergeants and Corporals and told them to get on with it.

It is a fact, whatever romantic notions may exist, that the Warrant Officers and Sergeants are the persons who, in the long run, hold a unit together. As Prisoners-of-War all of these were expected, and required, legally, by the enemy to undertake physical work, whether in their speciality or not. Officers on the other hand are not so obliged (under the Geneva Convention). Therefore even more responsibility fell on the non-commissioned officers — sergeants and sergeant-majors.

In a medical unit such as ours, things are a little different. Almost all the Commissioned Officers are doctors, called up for the duration, interested principally in medicine and surgery, and not in soldiering. They therefore, did work, following their laudable profession as required — and generally **only** as required. In other words, the chain of command, the organisation of the unit, was unchanged from that of peacetime, or phoney war in England. Added to this, before we had gone overseas I had been a buffer between the highest and the lowest and it was no wonder that when we became prisoners the 'other ranks' as they are called should turn to me for help and even advice. I felt like a very young 'uncle' when a man would come to me to tell me of his worries about his wife, or his future employment, or the unfair way he was being treated by someone else. Whether my advice was sound I know not. My principal tenet of belief at that time, which I used to impress on all who sought help was. "We have reached the lowest point in our lives, physically, emotionally and mentally. We have two possibilites — to live or to die. If we live then that is the greatest hurdle overcome. If we die, we have no need to worry." It seemed to comfort them.

Order for move to Thailand

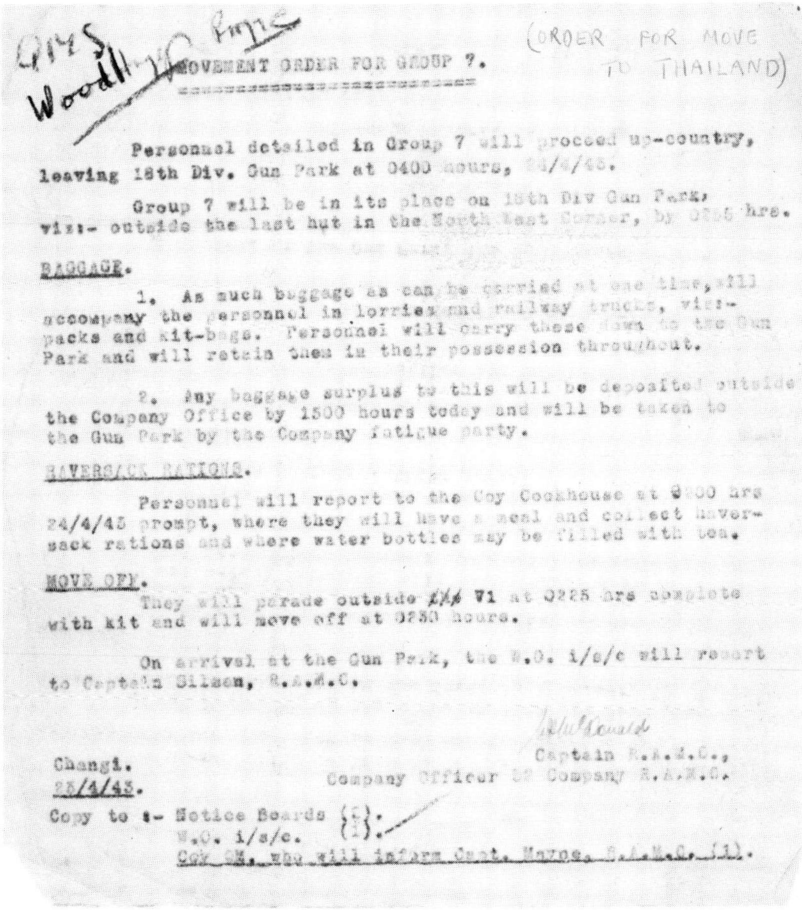
QMS Woodl[illegible] [illegible]

(ORDER FOR MOVE TO THAILAND)

MOVEMENT ORDER FOR GROUP 7.

Personnel detailed in Group 7 will proceed up-country, leaving 18th Div. Gun Park at 0400 hours, 24/4/43.

Group 7 will be in its place on 18th Div Gun Park, viz:- outside the last hut in the North East Corner, by 0[illegible] hrs.

BAGGAGE.

1. As much baggage as can be carried at one time, will accompany the personnel in lorries and railway trucks, viz:- packs and kit-bags. Personnel will carry these down to the Gun Park and will retain them in their possession throughout.

2. Any baggage surplus to this will be deposited outside the Company Office by 1500 hours today and will be taken to the Gun Park by the Company fatigue party.

HAVERSACK RATIONS.

Personnel will report to the Coy Cookhouse at 0200 hrs 24/4/43 prompt, where they will have a meal and collect haversack rations and where water bottles may be filled with tea.

MOVE OFF.

They will parade outside ~~[illegible]~~ V1 at 0225 hrs complete with kit and will move off at 0250 hours.

On arrival at the Gun Park, the W.O. i/c will report to Captain Silman, R.A.M.C.

Changi.
23/4/43.

[signature]
Captain R.A.M.C.,
Company Officer [illegible] Company R.A.M.C.

Copy to :- Notice Boards (2).
W.O. i/c. (1).
Coy QM, who will inform Capt. Mayne, R.A.M.C. (1).

9 *The March up Country 1943*

Dream and Reality

SO I woke during that day with the sun shining but great masses of clouds banking in the distant sky. There seemed to be some spare time — not necessary yet to do another medical round. Suddenly I realised that this was probably the most eventful period of my life — an adventure without much pleasure but full of incident, and revealing painfully what man could do to man, and how some reacted.

Childhood, youth, home, England, the Territorial Army, the War, and the captivity — a great picture painted on a mad canvas hung from the ceiling to the floor half-way across the room; reflecting in a distorted manner what had brought me there; hiding behind the unknown duration of the captivity, the half guessed at horrors still to come and the awful uncertainty of not seeing an end. There were going to be happenings that should not be forgotten. I **must** live, I **would** live, there must be an end.

So on to one's feet, do the rounds, a word of encouragement here, a sharper note there, prod and push spirit back into those too easily wanting to give up. Fall in; shuffle indeterminately across the flat and reasonable going of the staging camp; back into the track through the jungle, now rapidly narrowing, with no real daylight and rapidly complete darkness after sunset; and the first few drops of heavy rain; refreshing for a few minutes; then torrential. The march must end . . .

* * * * *

Writing on 30th April *"Left gun park Changi four a.m. 24.4.43 on Saturday, for Singapore in lorries.* [*We were put on to what we thought were cattle trucks, but probably were only goods trucks made of steel; they were enclosed with sliding doors on each side. Twenty-eight men went into each truck which meant that we could not all lie down at one time and indeed it was difficult for us to sit down without our knees up under our chins. There were frequent stops on the way for necessities of nature and for brew-ups, and what this amounted to was racing up to the front of the train, getting some water out of the boiler of the engine and racing back again, and putting in a handful of tealeaves. People who were really unwell had to endure it although the rest of us tried to make them more comfortable. The diary goes on:*]

[The figures in square brackets [1] *in the diary have been added since it was written and the previous map prepared, so that the reader may locate the camps.]*

Twenty-eight men per truck plus marching order and kit bags. Travelled by train Singapore to Bampong, [1] *Thailand, we think through Bangkok. Extremely hot during day, agonisingly cramping floor space, sixteen feet by six feet. Cold at night. Terrible rough journey. Unable to lie down comfortably. Malays and some Thais pleasant and helpful with food. Intolerable walk from station at Bampong to camp* [1A] *(Non Pladuk). Almost collapsed under weight of kit bag. Arrived four p.m. on 28th — meal which was only the sixth in the five days. Japanese (Tenko) number and medical inspection. Kit searched and nips stole my lighter. Had to dump a lot of kit for next march. Sold some for Thai dollars. Good night's sleep. Left eleven p.m. 29th in march order only. Goodbye kit. Marched seventeen miles, feet sore, no blisters.*

* * * * *

As though the four day cattle truck journey was not enough, this was the beginning of an ordeal no one could have contemplated or imagined. The fantastically long march, or rather trudge and slog, through the beginning of the monsoons, flooded streams and inches and sometimes feet of mud.

It all started off hopefully and optimistically along a road which had been at least partially metalled and I suppose in the early part of the night we talked and maybe even sang and whistled because I remember that it was still fine; the monsoon had not quite started. Men made temporary friends, sometimes a pair and sometimes three, but very seldom four in a group, and they tended to stay close together at all times in an animal instinct for the protection of the herd. We had had a very tiring journey and very little sleep and not much food, and to say we were exhausted, because after all we were very under nourished, would be an understatement.

However, we set off marching with packs heavier than they should have been, into the night and the jungle. I remember there were three of us, and as the night and the march wore on (and that first night was a distance of seventeen miles) our legs moved automatically, our minds to a very large extent were blank and fatigue crept down our foreheads until the eyelids drooped. I was on the outside of the right, my two friends on my left, and the middle man suddenly started wandering — staggering — in a general forward direction from side to side as though drunk. I realised he had in fact fallen asleep and from then on the man in the middle, with arms linked through the two on the outside, slept as he walked for perhaps ten minutes at a time. Then places were changed so that each might have this partial refreshment and release from the overpowering fatigue.

The map and the diagrammatic route of the march

Throughout captivity, and especially during and after the various expeditions to Siam in connection with the building of the railway, many Officers and men had maps of one sort or another. Some were made up by soldiers as they marched or moved about. Some were cribbed from Japanese maps being used in constructing the railway or pioneering the road. This is my own drawing torn up once and then stuck crudely together again:

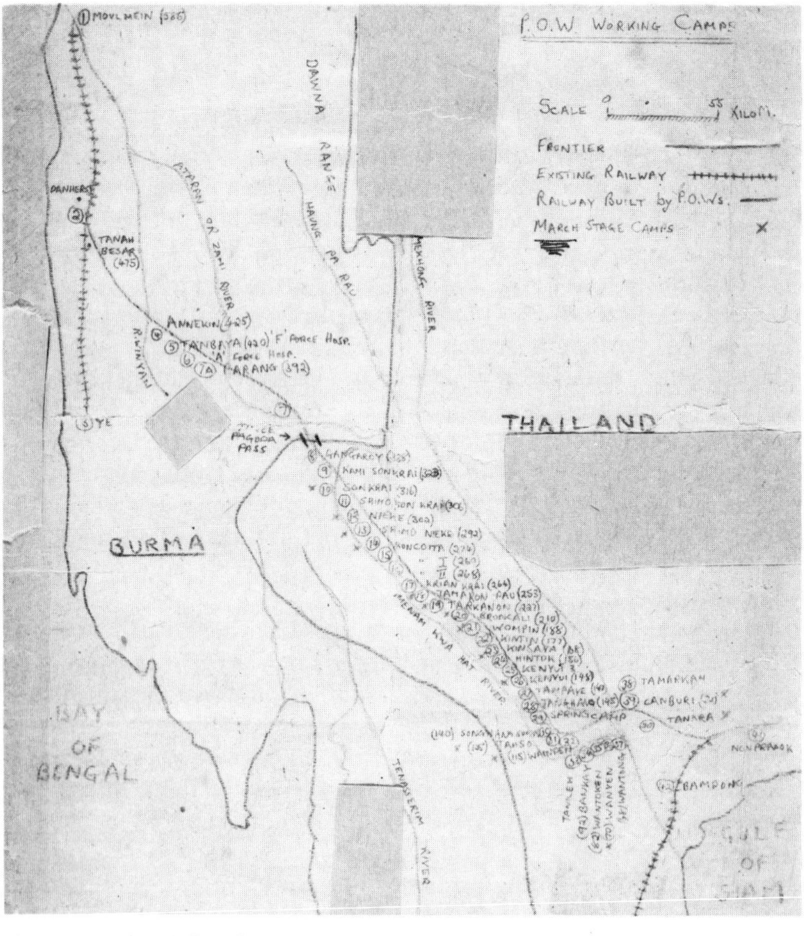

For a more detailed and accurate map — See Appendix

The diary goes on:

Great abdominal pain five to seven a.m. Bought meal from Thais at staging camp. [2] [*Taruanoi, Torowa, and Tawara*]. *Had bathe in river — dog tired. Bought Thai food in canteen — had some cover to sleep under but slept only two hours. Lousy meals and hard medical work. Nips have racket for taking heavy kit forward. Only carrying small pack tonight. Had about twenty hours sleep in eight days. Left this camp small kit only, 30th. Arrived thirty-six hours rest camp Camburi* [*Kanchanabri*] [3]."

May 1st "*Nine a.m. Had to live in jungle scrub, bathe in afternoon first. Started raining. Rained until midnight. Slept in lean-to and ground sheet. Very cramped little sleep. Next day sunny but no sleep. Off twelve midnight. Hard march all through the jungle carrying kit. Arrived day camp near river 3rd* [*Wompah*] [4]. *Very pleasant but still in jungle, one hours sleep. Off at nine p.m. Heavy packs by bullock cart, rest of kit on back. Arrived thirty-six hours camp on morning 4th* [*Wonyon*] [5]. *Still some Thais for selling food etc. Some rain but reasonable sleep. One man beaten by Japs. Crossed river by wooden bridge* [*Tadan Bridge*], *Arrived* [*Cantonburri — Taso*] [6] *camp on May 6th. Very large lot of troops. Very heavy going during night owing to rain. Forded two rivers. Very depressing camps. Still bivouacking in forest.*

* * * * *

On most nights the usual pattern was this. Night fell at about eight p.m. and the Japanese would call a Tenko (a roll call). We would assemble usually in rain in some kind of ragged order and then count ourselves and let them count us until they were satisfied that we were all there; apart from those who had died during the day. We would move off and the dark, smelly, depressing, dripping jungle would close about us. The track was barely wide enough for two and often narrowed down to a width that only one man could comfortably negotiate, so rapid was the growth of jungle plants in spite of the passage of many men.

Sometimes false hope would be raised by the track widening so that two or three could walk abreast, although walk is a euphemism. The ground had been virgin jungle and had been trod by many men and even perhaps some vehicles, as for example bullock carts and animals into a morass of mud ankle deep, shin deep and even on one or two occasions above the knees. The bare portions of the body and even those covered by clothes would often be whipped with sharp and scratchy or pointed thorns, twigs or branches because young bamboo cuts like a knife, and many a bamboo cut killed a man by becoming infected. The darkness was almost complete because of the monsoon clouds, the high over-powering and over-bearing jungle and the rain, only occasional glimpses of one's companions were possible.

Often it was safer to hold grimly on to the back of the groundsheet or cape, whatever the man in front was wearing and for the man behind you to do the same. If you fell at least someone knew and might be able to help you up.

Combined with this there were insects. The ever-present mosquito, which seemed not to mind the rain, and more filthy than all, in the myriad little streams which ran along the jungle floor, and through which tired legs splashed, there were leeches and no way of removing them except by brushing them off, a most unwise thing to do; but where was the match, fire or the lighter which could be used to make them release their grip?

* * * * *

The diary goes on:

"Left evening 6th. More rain, heavy going. Arrived 7th, small camp [*Kenyui*] [7]. *Poor washing facilities, hopeless latrine facilities. Left on evening 7th. Another heavy night carrying men on stretchers. Arrived morning 8th at bigger camp* [*Kinsayo*] [8]. *Our road and other roads in course of construction. Meals are atrocious — no Thais to buy things from. Long distance from rivers. Slept reasonably. May 9th, Sunday. Completed this diary to date. Very difficult to keep track of days and dates. Cut my foot yesterday. General fatigue terrible. That was thirty-six hour camp. Left there evening May 9th arrived in depressing little camp morning of 10th.* [*Wompin*] [9]. *Slept little. Food worse but river near. Off again and arrived in thirty-six hour camp Tuesday morning May 11th. There is a Jap Sergeant known locally as 'Hitler'* [*Tarkanon*] [10] *in charge extremely officious. Everything is done by parades and saluting. Food just as bad but at last we can sleep if it doesn't rain.*

Review of the position; left Changi eighteen days ago travelled about 1,200 miles now in Thailand close to Burma frontier. Altogether we have marched so far nine nights about 120-130 miles. We have three meals a day of rice, quarter pint, alleged veg. water, half a dozen dices of vegetable. Only drink is river water when chlorinated. We usually have a two or three hour halt in the middle of the night to sleep after we have done our medical chores. Am very tired indeed but so far have not fallen down. If anyone falls out on the line of march they have to be carried. When it rains we are ankle to knee deep in mud. Three of us have bound together and we have bivouacked in the woods under ground sheets. I have about 1/6th of my kit with me, the rest depends on the Japs. To get salt would be a luxury."

It is difficult to convey the utter despair and despondency which pervaded our spirits on this inhuman march. Only our hatred of our captors, our fatalistic acceptance of every hardship saved us from just giving up physically and mentally.

We would be paraded just before dark and counted. We had all our possessions on our persons; strapped on, tied on, hanging round our necks. Our clothes were ragged, filthy, and wet. The rain poured down. We had gone many days with only one meal in the day, or at most two, and consisting of plain white rice, alleged vegetable water, and black tea. We had sores from marching and our chafing clothes; we had foot rot from the mud, and insect bites and stings.

So we set off. Night fell. So did the rain. In the early part of the night we cursed — later we did not have even the desire to do that. We would march, stumble, flounder, wade, trudge and slog on. Perhaps there would be a 'camp' where perhaps again we might be given a cup of hot water. It was always hot. Presumably because it had been boiled.

Whenever there was a stop, the medics, Officers, N.C.Os, and men had first to see if there were any sick needing urgent attention, (and there always were) any men who simply needed encouragement or bullying to carry on; any stretcher parties or helping shoulders to organise. Then we would line up for our water. Often there was none left. So off again, sometime in the small hours but time stood still — there was only the eternal night and the eternal jungle. Perhaps an hour or sometimes two, before dawn, after about ten hours on the road — what road? the way, the journey, the trek, we would come into what the guards called a 'rest' camp. It might be occupied solely by Japanese, or Thais as well, and sometimes our own troops. We would be issued with hot water, hot vegetable juice, rice.

First for the R.A.M.C. however, was the treatment of the troops; pricking blisters, binding wounds in rags, perhaps extracting splinters of bamboo or other objects, administering to the sick. Only then could we queue for our rations. We would sit on the soaking ground, under the steady downpour in luxury if there was cover of a sort. Then we would try to build some sort of cover, with banana leaves, a corner of groundsheet — anything and crawl in and sleep; often two or three or more men huddled together for warmth, and to try to dispel the damp from their bones.

Dawn would come unnoticed, if briefly the sun shone things might be laid out to dry. On waking after three, four or five hours sleep there would be 'make and mend' trying to repair the ravages of the night past and prepare for the night to come. Some chance of mixing and talking then the evening meal, the parade and 'All men march'.

Sometimes it was a thirty-six hour and not a twelve hour stopover but we often were not told this until well into the first day so there was little chance to plan, and perhaps build, for a longer stay. We forgot what life was like continually on the move, and wet, hungry and filthy.

Many men today still suffer the rheumatics brought on by this experience.

* * * * *

May 12th *"Wednesday. Slept fairly well had bathe in river early morning, very refreshing. We expected an extra rest here but I am afraid we shall move on tonight."*

May 13th *"Thursday. We moved last night and arrived at usual day camp slight improvement in food [Tarkanon]* [11]."

May 14th *"Friday. Another day camp, [Tampranpat]* [12] *that means tonight is the third night's march in succession and the jungle is very boring but we occasionally see wild banana trees now a good sign. All these camps are for the purpose of building roads and railways. We sometimes see elephants but very few natives. We are extremely fatigued and very thin. Only hope we can keep together in the hospital. We have marched eleven nights and covered about one hundred and fifty miles in a north or north westerly direction."*

May 15th *"Saturday. Arrived in hutted camp. [Koncuita]* [13]. *No roofs to huts. Really fagged out and had to be helped in. Had some diarrhoea. Stayed in camp for night. Reasonable sleep on bamboo floor. Stayed in camp all day. Next party did not arrive. Large party of Australians moved out."*

May 16th *"Sunday. Moved in evening two hundred yards down the road because Japs evacuated the camp. Many locals have died. Seven in twenty-four hours? Cholera. Had Japanese Cholera injection. Slept under tent pure luxury. [Upper Koncuita]* [14]."

May 17th *"Monday. Early in morning moved again two hundred yards down road to camp in jungle. [Upper Tiemonta]* [15]. *Going to stay night but 196 arrived and am going along with them but am feeling very exhausted. Our last six meals have consisted of onions and rice only. The food* **must** *improve. We believe tonights march is the last. We are only about one hundred and fifty miles from Rangoon."*

May 18th *"Tuesday. Arrived in camp which is alleged to be base, which turned out to be Shimo Nieke [Lower Nikki]* [16]. *The hospital will probably be here. Our rations are good but scanty. Two men have died from Cholera. Very very hungry."*

10 *From the Cholera Camp to the Frontier*

Medical Nightmare

MAY 19th 1943 *"Wednesday. Trains 7, 8, 9, marched out leaving me behind to look after hospital stores. The Officers as usual commandeered the hospital and all the stores. I am to endeavour to combat them. Another man died today from Cholera. The bodies are burned on huge piles of logs and tree trunks".*

* * * * *

That entry includes the words 'The Officers as usual commandeered the hospital and all the stores. I am to endeavour to combat them'. These were words written at the time — in the knowledge that they could well be seen by others so one can be sure they were bitterly true.

The system of command and discipline has been explained before and it resulted in officers from combatant units (all except the R.A.M.C. and Dental Corps) being idle most of the time. These Officers, mostly of junior rank would, in camp, with no duties, literally try to corner all the comforts — the hut with a decent roof; medical supplies and so on. They behaved in this way off and on during the whole of captivity and most officers were heartily detested by their own troops. The more senior an Officer was, the more likely that he was fair and above board.

The entry says, 'I am to endeavour to combat them'. Note the words. When my own R.A.M.C. Officers left they said in their own words. "For God's sake keep these bastards away from our stores." Life seemed very unfair to me but I did combat them; and I spent much of my Prisoner-of-War life as a rebel because of this. I could not agree with those who shrugged and said. "Well, they are Officers," as though this excused their behaviour. Let me make it clear at once, that this did not apply to Officers of the R.A.M.C. They are in any case, all or almost all, doctors in civilian life; they were called upon to cure medically without medicines, and to undertake surgery in the most primitive conditions, with inadequate tools. Their behaviour, from the Lt. Cols down to the Assistant Surgeon Anglo-Indians was never in doubt. I felt aggrieved with them sometimes for having to undertake the disciplinary tasks which were really their responsibility as the entry which started all this shows.

May 20th *"Thursday. Diarrhoea in the night. Train 10 marched in. Some progress in regard to stores. These camps are built entirely of bamboo. No roofs to huts. Beds are on floor of bamboo. This diary one year old."*

May 21st *"Friday. Evening. Worst twenty-four hours I have ever experienced. Acute diarrhoea and a go of malaria. Rained all last night and as the cover in the hospital is inadequate, I got wet through. Mild cramps at noon."*

May 22nd *"Saturday. A little better but still diarrhoea. The last six meals have consisted of entirely rice and togay.* [*bean shoots*]"

May 23rd *"Sunday. Diarrhoea continues. Very much rain. A little cover."*

May 24th *"Monday. A decent night. Fairly fine day. Everyone depressed. I feel a little better."*

May 29th *"Settling down under appalling conditions. No roofs. Everyone has diarrhoea. Open latrines. Food consisting of rice and a little bean soup or something else. Only a dirty stream to wash in. All water chlorinated. Raining all the time, but still cheerful. I had fever last night, better today. Sore from sleeping on bamboo."*

June 3rd *"Thursday. I spent a most unpleasant week. Constant embarrassing diarrhoea, violent pain, headache, disease, continually damp because there is no roof on the huts and it rains all the time. Woke one morning with cholera symptoms — rice water vomit and stools — refused to accept it."*

* * * * *

Life is a matter of will — the will to live. Without a mind that says I will live there is death, and however serious the symptoms, however debilitating the result, however little hope there is, faith, the faith of mind over the body is the most powerful factor in effecting a cure.

In the several life-times of experience I went through as a prisoner this occurred on three occasions and perhaps the first was the most frightening. I had been at Shimo Nike, which had been called the Cholera Camp, for some time and had been beset with constant diarrhoea with internal cramps and the rigors of malaria. I had been doing my job as a qualified nursing orderly and with an obligation because of my rank to set an example, which meant constantly nursing cholera cases. Although my own ill health — and indeed that of all the medical staff, would have made us candidates for any hospital in England.

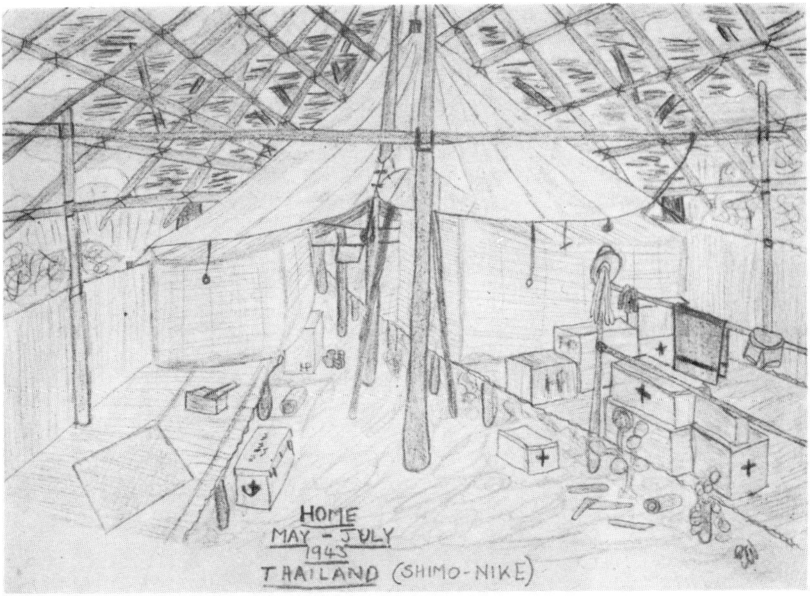

Sketch by the author

The following description is not for the squeamish, but it must be understood in order to know what the hundreds of men who died from this terrible disease of cholera went through. One morning waking up stiff in body from lying all night on the bamboo platform, I was suddenly taken with violent cramps and without any control, vomited on to my bed-space, a cloudy white fluid. The first symptoms of cholera are often intestinal cramps and vomiting and diarrhoea. Both stools and the vomit look like water which rice is cooked in — a milky white fluid. The incidence of these attacks becomes more frequent, the rigors turning into immense spasms; prostration follows: skin goes grey blue and clammy and the whole body sinks into itself. Very often a man's voice will change to a hoarse whisper, temperature drops, pulse almost disappears and muscular pain in the legs and thighs becomes almost unbearable.

When a man saw what he had vomited and what he was passing he *knew* that without adequate treatment which we did not have, he had at most forty-eight hours to live.

I too, should have died; but I refused to accept it. I lay on that filthy bamboo platform through the day with fortunately no one particularly near me, and no one wanting to get near me, while the rain poured down outside and in through the roof. There were moments when consciousness left me and others when I thought with a clarity quite beyond the powers of the mind in a normal healthy body. But as the day wore on I vomited less and less frequently, and it seemed that all that could have drained out of me had done so and I fell into an exhausted unconsciousness.

I woke next morning with no pain but a light-headiness due to complete starvation, yet with the knowledge of being given a new life.

* * * * *

June 8th *"Tuesday. We have a lot of rain every day. Today we had a real monsoon downpour. Conditions steadily become worse but I live! Rations are often short because of the indescribable state of the roads. The camp is slowly being evacuated to the next one, Nieke, but I must remain behind until all the stores have moved. The Nips have made a complete balls of this move. Seven thousand British and Australian POW's were moved from Changi to help them build road and railway in Western Thailand. We have been here three weeks but owing to the fatiguing train journey and the dreadful march one thousand are scattered all along the route sick. In six camps here some two thousand to three thousand are sick; all told to date there have been two hundred deaths."*

June 21st *"Monday. There seems no chance of us moving. We have no tobacco and am very miserable without. Working very hard."*

June 27th *"Sunday. Still here but by all accounts better off than at Nieke. Everything here is bamboo. We use it for fires, bedpans, cut longitudinally, bowls and buckets cut across, labels, tablets, gravestone and cremation caskets. In addition our huts are made of it entirely including the floor (raised up) on each side of the alleyway (mud). This floor is also our bed. Our conversation here is firstly food, then drink, release, action, the news and women in that order. It still rains most of each day. We hope in two days for the end of the monsoon season. I write this with a pen that I have found. My own set long ago went the way of all kit".*

* * * * *

I was left without a medical officer (doctor) just myself, a sergeant and I think about ten other ranks all R.A.M.C. who were reasonably fit, or fit according to our standards then, and approximately fifty cases of cholera or dysentery or malaria or whatever — but very sick men, many of them in a terminal stage of illness — and one guard.

The following illustrations are from photographs which were made available to members of the Far East Prisoner-of-War Association fairly soon after the War. They were also reproduced in the British Medical Journal (published by the British Medical Association) under a general heading 'Medical Experiences in Japanese Captivity — E.E. Dunlop' in October 1946. If acknowledgements are due to anyone for the re-printing in this book of these photographs I at once do so and express my gratitude to them. The B.M.J. Article was written by Lieut-Col E.E. Dunlop M.S., F.R.C.S. of the Australian Army Medical Corps and he is mentioned in other books written by ex-POWs. I do not remember having the privilege of meeting him. The pictures are captioned with my own wording and convey perhaps more easily than words, the conditions up and down the camp sites on the railway and road.

Pictures obtained from Far East Prisoner of War Association (London) in 1948

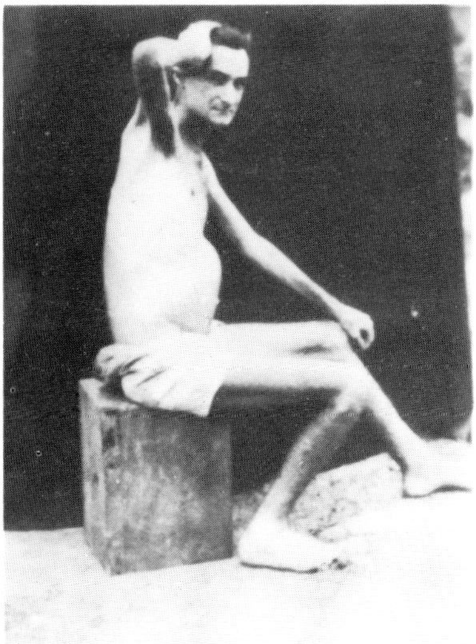

"Wet" Beri-Beri

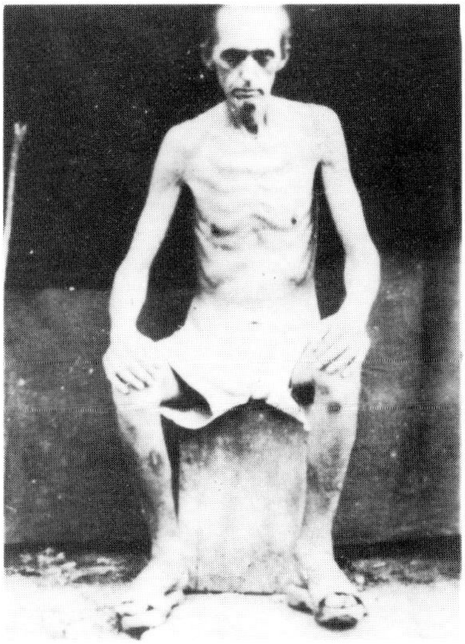

Acute case of malnutrition

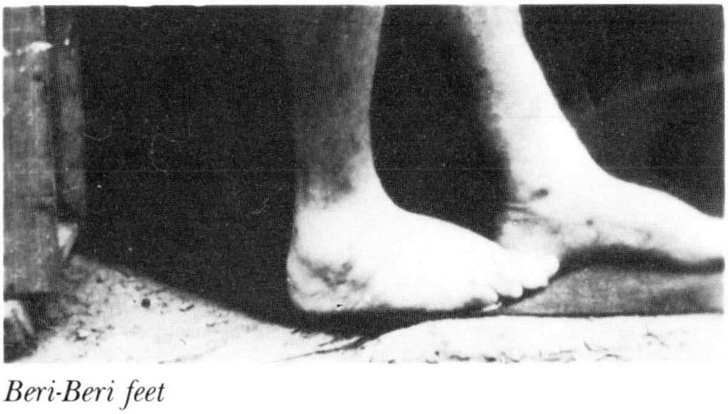

Beri-Beri feet

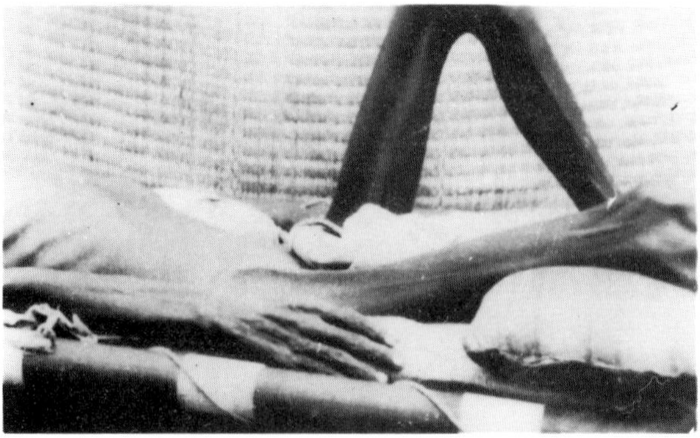

Cholera

Tropical ulcer,
bone showing

Temuang camp

Kanburi hospital

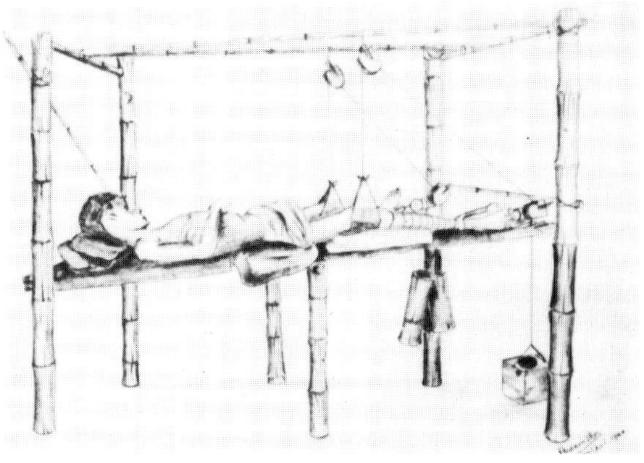

Jungle traction

Some uses for bamboo

To wake sore and stiff and drawn from incessant night diarrhoea; to try to perform some kind of ablutions; to line up for plain white rice and coloured water, to stand in ranks for tenko, to be marched out of the camp to the work site to the latest hare-brained scheme of wooden trestle over a terrifying gorge, or excavating manually vast quantities of earth and mud from a cutting; to put up with this for eight or ten hours, a meagre rest midday and unnourishing food; to stagger back to camp in the evening; to try to wash, to feed, to sink down on one's bed of split bamboo. This was the lot of the N.C.Os and men of the combatant units in the camp; luckier still if they did not eventually need our ministrations for anything more serious than the catalogue of endemic diseases common to all. In Shimo Nieke however, I had only the relics of such a camp the others having moved on. It was not surprising therefore, that during the course of the next week or two a lot of the men died — there was nothing we could do to save them. One or two started getting better, and we slowly contracted the camp, burning huts as we left them, and withdrawing into an enclave or ghetto so as to limit the area of infection. It could have been a scene from a primitive war.

* * * * *

July 13th *"Tuesday. Day before yesterday moved all stores and patients, all staff into previous Nip guard hut. Very trying day complicated by rain. Sgt Jim Innes and I shifted the whole of the medical store. It was nice to sleep under a decent attapp* [*dried palm fronds*] *roof. Expected to move from this camp Lower Nieke to Nieke proper. Had day's rest. Did a little writing. Decided to adopt a different name for Pithecanthropus Erectus (book) which I have just started writing. Today marched to Nieke carrying kit which had become somewhat heavier. Going very bad. Knee deep in mud in some places. Had to ford two streams. Fine conditions here, much the same but better roofing. Reasonably well received by Australians here. Better of course by the British people. Mr. Sindon marched with me — both very tired and a little stiff."*

THAILAND TREK

Far away in cities,
Where the men lead normal lives,
And sip and taste their whiskies
While joking with their wives;
They who talk of hardship,
And of hunger, thirst, and death,
They've never known the real thing
They're merely wasting breath.

Man has never hungered
Till he craved a dish of rice,
And swallowed smelly dried fish
And could have eaten twice;
Let him trek at night-time
Have an aching void within,
And nought from dusk till noonday
Just starving — with a grin!

Let him eat the same food
But just once or twice a day,
And needing something tasty
To help the meals away.
Let him have a craving
For some meat or savoury stew,
No hotel food will tempt him,
Give him a steak or two.

Man has never thirsted,
Till he's marched through blinding dust,
And the rotting smell of jungle,
Has filled him with disgust.
Chest and head near bursting,
With the blood at temples tight,
His sweating body crying,
For cooling soothing night.

Let him drink with avid longing,
Of the water from a stream,
With slimy muddy bottom,
Yet taste a wine supreme.
Water chlorinated
With a taste that's ne'er forgot,
Or boiled till merely tasteless
And drunk while steaming hot.

Man has never wearied,
Till he's marched a hundred miles,
And seventy more above that,
In winding double files.
Marched at nights with pack on,
Through the mire and mud and slush,
In heat and wind and rainstorm;
Alternate stop, and rush.

Let him wade through torrents
Of water wide and deep,
With legs of lead and footsore
And eyes that drop with sleep.
See the man before him,
Like a phantom in the rain;
To sink knee deep in potholes
And rise and fall again.

Man has never noticed,
The cadaverous touch of death,
Till friends have died around him
With laboured gasping breath;
Fevers strange and sudden,
And the scourge of diarrhoea,
Of cholera sores and dengue --
Will give him cause to fear.

Let him see some crosses,
Made of bamboo poles and string,
And hear the solemn 'Last Post'
A common, mournful, thing.
Tell him of his comrades
Whom he's known on every side,
And watch him shrug his shoulders,
When told that they have died.

Man has never rested
Till he's dropped upon the ground,
And lain where he has fallen
To sleep the clock round;
Sit with shoulders forward,
Just to ease the pain
Of heavy pack or kitbag,
All sodden with the rain.

Let him take his groundsheet
And spread it in the scrub,
Not heeding flies and insects,
Too tired to scratch or rub.
Showers of rain upon him,
And the drippings from the trees;
The blazing sun by daytime,
At night the chilling breeze.

I have known all these things
With those few I marched beside,
Who slipped and trudged and floundered,
But kept their native pride;
We know the truth of hardship,
And we know the death and thirst;
But they could never beat us,
We'd see Them . . . first.

17.7.43

July 14th *"Quiet today. Started on my book work. Slept under net and well."*

July 15th *"Further quiet day shaking down."*

July 20th *"Tuesday. On Sunday I was sent to Shimo Nieke again to collect all medical stores and patients. Covered the five miles down in reasonable time but going very bad. Loaded packs of Red Cross food and Jim and I started off with a pannier between us on poles. We had to carry twenty sleeping mats the same way. Rained hard all the time. Mats got heavier."*

11 *Number One Medicine*

(What follows here is a true short story I wrote for a competition soon after my return home. It amplifies the diary entry for July 20th in the previous chapter. The story was unpublished).

HIS name was Toyama. He was a Korean, in the days when Korea was one country and part of the Japanese Empire. The thrifty Japanese had left him in charge, in sole charge, of Shimo Nieke, a collection of tumbledown bamboo huts in a hard-won clearing on the track which was to become the Burma railway. Shimo Nieke was to be a base camp, a sort of Clapham Junction of the 'Great Northern Railway of the Greater East Asia Co-prosperity Sphere', as they called it.

But high sounding names and the single-mindedness of the Japanese could not replace at a moment's notice the lives lost along each yard of the track. Base was moved a few kilometres further on, and left behind at Shimo Nieke like the flotsam on a deserted beach, about fifty men for whom the sole official purpose and design was to die. Not from cholera, since forty-eight hours to make peace is all that is left when the vomiting starts. No, mostly dysentery, malaria, vicious bone destroying tropical ulcers and the scourge of the rice-eater beri-beri.

The frugal Japanese left one Korean to guard these relics of the British Empire — his name was Toyama and he was afraid. Perhaps nineteen or twenty years old, no more, he found himself five hundred miles from any semblance of civilisation, surrounded by jungle where apart from the blood soaked track a day's march was a machete-won mile of ground. With him for companions were fifty white men — men who hated his guts for all he knew. His war had lasted through China to Malaya and from Borneo to the Phillipines. He believed passionately that the Nipponese Army would win but he was afraid. Afraid because he was only a Korean, a very third-rate soldier in a despised contingent, and because his beloved country was under the heel of the Japanese and would remain so when the war was over.

He was most afraid because of his loneliness. At night when the jungle served as an amplifier for sounds not of this world he lay alone in the little guard room, snug enough with its attapp roof, and thought his bitter thoughts.

He would do what he could for us. Blandishments and appeals would bring forth a few more tougay beans, a handful more of rice, to alleviate a little the sufferings of those who writhed in intestinal agony or lay passive bloated obscenely to twice their size with the watery death of beri-beri. He would come into the places we dignified by the name of 'wards' and stand at the end of the mud run between the bamboo flooring and watch us silently as we, my four companions and I, did our pitiful best to relieve the sufferings of our comrades. We at least had the high purpose of our nursing calling to armour us against the madness of mental loneliness.

Then one day he came to me. He stood and gazed at me over our two solitary medical panniers.

He said. "Me — " pointing at his abdomen, "geri-geri."

My friend Jim, the chemist, growled in his Scot's voice. "And serve you ruddy well right."

I shrugged. What could we do for a Korean in Japanese uniform with dysentery? What *should* we do if we could? And should we? I felt fierce delight that this little brown man, this man who might have had our friends' blood on his hands should be smitten with the perpetual scourge. My thinking parts said 'Pity him' as you would anyone who is sick. My year already of imprisonment, and the years that were yet to come, told me to rejoice at his downfall.

Jim and I talked freely in front of him. Our communication with our guards was always a mixture of pidgin English, Malay and the odd word of Japanese. He could not follow our rapid idiomatic flow. We gave him a home-made preparation of Kaolin which though rudimentary is a great intestinal binder — but could only alleviate in very small measure and is in no wise a cure for dysentery.

But when the night fell and to the noise of the unceasing monsoon rain there was added the noise of the nocturnal jungle, Jim and I were not so sure.

Jim said. "It's all very well but suppose he really has got dysentery and not just diarrhoea. Suppose he gets worse."

I said. "Probably shamming — haven't we got worries enough."

"He may be — just wants sympathy — or more probably some opium — and calls it medicine."

"Could be — hope you're right."

"Suppose he really falls sick — helplessly ill — will you get anyone to nurse him?"

"Should I?"

"I dunno — I dunno at all — after all he is a ruddy Jap."

"Korean."

"Same thing."

"Then maybe we'll let him die eh?"

"Yes — serve him right."

"And peace perfect peace will visit this camp."

Jim suddenly sat up. "But would it? — what about the mob up the river. They'd be down here like a pack of wolves. If the Jap sergeant came down and found Toyama dead, what would he say?"

I sat up too, this could be serious. "What's more important, what would he *do?* Look Jim. Suppose Toyama died. We couldn't bury him or burn him — we'd have to darn well keep him till someone came down to us. Or else we'd have to send a man, no two men, up to the next camp to tell them. Ten chances to one, if they ever got there on their own they'd be shot out of hand as escapees."

"We couldn't send anyone."

"No — we'd have to wait for that blasted Gunso to come down — and it might be days — and Toyama would lie around stinking even if we parcelled him up away from the flies."

"That's not all you know. They'd blame us — even if they knew darn well that he died of disease. Someone would be losing his head."

"Do you think so?"

"No — not really — though I wouldn't put it past them. What would happen is that there'd be a few beating-ups and rations reduced — the full treatment."

"Then he'd better get better again."

"Let's wait till the morning. He'll be along fast enough."

And he was, but only just. He tottered into the hut and clung weakly to the support pole in the middle. With a face drained of colour, no rifle, his uniform disarranged he looked at us with eyes that had lost their fierceness.

He said. "Me — no good — number ten — geri-geri all night — benjo one hundred — you give me number one medicine."

Jim and I looked at him in consternation. He meant it. He so obviously had been up all night to and fro to the latrine. We had seen it all too many times before. In the few seconds between words we saw the awful possibilities that we'd talked about. The hideous consequences of letting this man die. The consequences not only to us and the medical orderlies but to the forty or so sick and dying men over there in the 'ward'.

It is difficult after this passage of time, with a full stomach, a comfortable home and fears only of nuclear explosions, to know just what really activated us. At the time I feel we rationalised the small impulse we had to help a fellow human by saying that the consequences of not helping him made it necessary. Membership of our Corps enjoined us to help the sick both friend and foe at all times, but it comes hard to tend your enemy. We had done so, we had no alternative back in the camps in Singapore but this seemed different. Powerless though we were we suddenly had power.

Whatever the motives we treated Toyama as best we could. It was pitifully poor treatment but our captors were to blame for keeping us criminally short of medical drugs and supplies.

The days passed. A few men died. A few others recovered somewhat. The largest number stayed as they were — hovering — a battleground for will-power against lethargy with life or death as the reward. Toyama improved but he hovered too. The hated Gunso and his patrol paid a visit. Toyama was able to walk round with them. The rain stopped a little. Toyama recovered. He came into our hut and stood looking at us. Nobody said anything. He went away without a word. He was relieved as our guard. A stranger took his place.

It must have been about a month later that the Japs decided to evacuate our camp — now only about thirty-five men. They sent down a small carrying party from the camp further on. Toyama was with them but he gave no sign of recognition. Six of these relatively fit men in parties each made stretchers or carrying chairs of bamboo and took away the pitiful remnants of our wards. Others carried bundles of plaited bamboo mats on poles slung between two shoulders — white slaves in a heathen jungle. Jim and I carried a medical pannier in the same fashion.

But we were both sick men. How sick we did not know. We too had malaria but it was with us all the time and as the easiest way to die was to lie down we had carried on with our work.

There was nothing heroic about it — it was self-preservation. Intestinal trouble was our constant companion. Our legs and wrists weeped in a myriad of tiny tropical sores. We joined in the caravan.

Monsoon rain has to be experienced to be believed and we were almost through the monsoon period. The narrow track carved out of the living jungle was a quagmire of mud — literally knee deep most of the way. We had no flesh on our bones and in spite of rags as pads the bamboo pole swaying and jogging with our uneven steps under the weighty pannier bit like a blunt axe into our shoulders. A hundred yards is a mile under such conditions. We lagged behind. A declivity of a few yards sent us stumbling to our knees to rise heavier by a few more pounds of mud. A slight incline brought us to the top gasping for breath. The column disappeared from view with Toyama bringing up the rear his rifle across his back.

I begged him for just five minutes rest when we reached a relatively drier patch. We both sat down. I could hardly get to my feet again. To lift the burden on to my raw shoulder was agony. To walk with it cruelty refined.

Toyama came back to see why we were so long. His brows were knit. He had again that crafty mean look we associated so well with yellow skin and slant eyes.

He used the word which all Japs used to indicate anger, displeasure and a command to get on with it more quickly.

"Kurra-kurra."

I really had had enough. I spread my hands in mock resignation. "Me finished." I said. "Dumme, dumme — no good — can't carry — finished."

In a rage Toyama unslung his rifle and grasping the barrel flexed it behind his head preparatory to aiming a blow at my head or shoulders. Comically I felt hurt — I remember feeling hurt at such base ingratitude — and I remember thinking that this was not a rational feeling. I said quickly before the blow could fall.

"You — geri-geri — me number one medicine — you better — remember?"

The arrested movement changed its direction. The rifle slowly came down to his side. "So-ka?" he breathed sibilantly, "so-ka — it is so — you number one." He looked at Jim and then at me. He bowed politely. "Arigato gozaimasu," he said — my genuine thanks.

He gave me his rifle to carry. He picked up my end of the load, and from then on took one end while Jim and I took the other together.

And so we came to camp.

Diary resumed:

July 21st *"Wednesday. I was bitten by a scorpion at Shimo Nieke but with no ill effects. Food here at Nieke proper is poor. Rice some beans sometimes a suspicion of dried Yak".*

July 25th *"Monday. A few days ago, Col. Huston arrived, a very good thing. The people here are being shaken up. Two nights ago an officer with cerebral malaria got up in the middle of the night and wandered off. The Nip Gestapo arrived and took superfluous particulars but there is at present no news of the poor devil. Yesterday there was an operation for appendectomy performed with skeleton instruments on a bamboo table in our bamboo hut. The man is progressing favourably. It rains 80% of the twenty-four hours and the river has risen six feet in a week. It is now a few inches from the level of the bank. Pay is in the offing but there is only a very perfunctory canteen arrangement with Nieke village. There is reason to believe that some patients and staff will be shortly moved to Burma to a new 'convalescent depot'."*

[There is a gap]

We were paid yesterday and have been able to buy Gula and milk at the canteen.

Also Jim Burge RASC who unloads barges at Nieke village proper bought for us Gula, tinned fish and cheroots at twenty-five cents each. Thai money only is accepted. A small force including Major Phillips and Fred Steward have left for Burma to establish a con. depot.

August 2nd *"August Bank Holiday and what a day. Warned yesterday at 15.00 that all stores were to be parked and myself and Mr. Sindon were to go into No. 2 camp. Left about eleven a.m. and arrived eight p.m.* [*Son Kurai*] [18]. *Rained most of the time. Roads very bad deep in mud and corduroy or flint roads very hard on feet. Arrived dead beat and slept fifteen to a bay in a hut i.e. touching all round. Slept well strangely enough. Felt well but tired this morning".*

August 3rd *"No effort yet been made to accommodate us more comfortably. Mr. Childs is in charge of the hospital. I do not think he has the spirit he once had. Meeting up again with some of my older friends. Very glad to see Haggy especially because of the loss of Taffy. Wild rumours here.* [*Working friends at the time.*]"

August 12th *"Conditions here are terrible. Ten deaths a day and the stink of ulcers is overpowering. Cholera has broken out at Nieke. Two men have been tied to a tree for forty-eight hours because one ran away from a working party and the other struck at Nip".*

Full size photograph of page of actual diary.

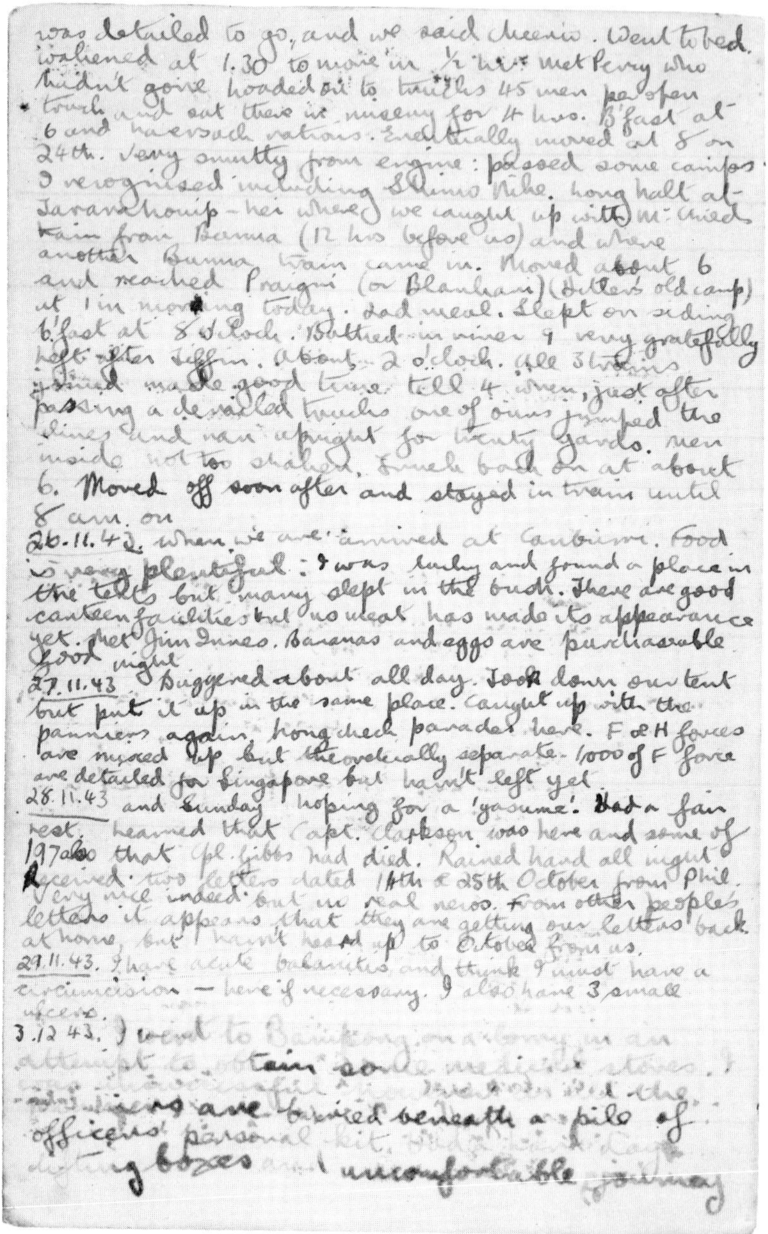

was detailed to go, and we said cheerio. Went to bed. wakened at 1.30 to move in ½ hr. Met Perry who hadn't gone. Loaded on to trucks 45 men per open truck and sat there in misery for 4 hrs. B'fast at 6 and haversack rations. Eventually moved at 8 on 24th. Very smutty from engine: passed some camps I recognised including Shimo Nike. Long halt at Taranchoup — where we caught up with Mc. Chied train from Burma (12 hrs before us) and where another Burma train came in. Moved about 6 and reached Praigni (or Blanham) (Hitler's old camp) at 1 in morning today. Bad meal. Slept on siding. B'fast at 8 o'clock. Bathed in river & very gratefully left after tiffin. About 2 o'clock. All 3 trains joined. made good time till 4 when, just after passing a derailed truck one of ours jumped the lines and ran upright for twenty yards. Men inside not too shaken. Truck back on at about 6. Moved off soon after and stayed in train until 8 am. on

26.11.43. when we are arrived at Kanburi. Food is very plentiful: I was lucky and found a place in the tents but many slept in the bush. There are good canteen facilities but no meat has made its appearance yet. Met Jim Innes. Bananas and eggs are purchasable. Good night

27.11.43 Buggered about all day. Took down our tent but put it up in the same place. Caught up with the panniers again. Long check parades here. F & H forces are mixed up but theoretically separate. 1,000 of F force are detailed for Singapore but haven't left yet

28.11.43 and Sunday hoping for a 'yasume'. Had a fair rest. Learned that Capt. Clarkson was here and some of 197 also that Cpl. Gibbs had died. Rained hard all night. Received two letters dated 14th & 25th October from Phil. Very nice indeed but no real news. From other people's letters it appears that they are getting our letters back at home, but I haven't heard up to October from us.

29.11.43. I have acute balanitis and think I must have a circumcision — here if necessary. I also have 3 small ulcers.

3.12.43. I went to Bankong on a lorry in an attempt to obtain some medical stores. I [illegible] the [illegible] are buried beneath a pile of officers' personal kit, [illegible] boxes and [illegible] uncomfortable journey

Full size photograph of page of actual diary.

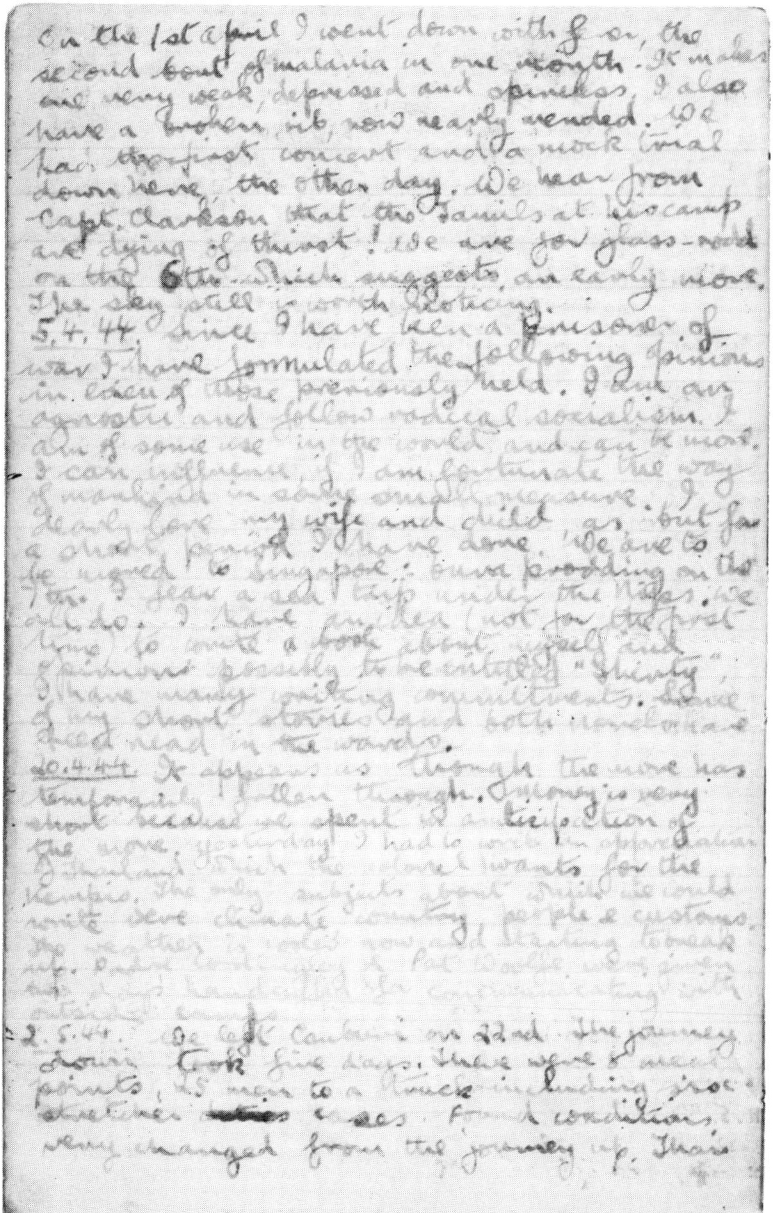
On the 1st April I went down with fever, the
second bout of malaria in one month. It makes
me very weak, depressed and spineless. I also
have a broken rib, now nearly mended. We
had the first concert and a mock trial
down here, the other day. We hear from
Capt. Clarkson that the Tamils at his camp
are dying of thirst! We are for glass-road(?)
on the 6th which suggests an early move.
The sky still is worth noticing.
5.4.44. Since I have been a prisoner of
war I have formulated the following opinions
in place of those previously held. I am an
agnostic and follow radical socialism. I
am of some use in the world and can be more.
I can influence, if I am fortunate, the way
of mankind in some small measure. I
dearly love my wife and child as but for
a short period I have done. We are to
be moved to Singapore: move prodding(?) on the
7th. I fear a sea trip under the Nips, we
all do. I have an idea (not for the first
time) to write a book about myself and
opinions possibly to be entitled "Thirty".
I have many writing commitments. Some
of my short stories and both novels have
been read in the wards.
20.4.44. It appears as though the move has
temporarily fallen through. Money is very
short because we spent it in anticipation of
the move. Yesterday I had to write an appreciation
of Thailand which the colonel wants for the
Kempis(?). The only subjects about which we could
write were climate, country, people & customs.
The weather is cooler now and starting to break
up. [illegible] Pat Wolfe was given
[illegible] handcuffed for communicating with
outside camps.
2.5.44. We left Canburi on 22nd. The journey
down took five days. There were 8 meal
points, 25 men to a truck including five
stretcher [illegible] cases. Food conditions
very changed from the journey up. Thais

12 *Ten must die*

NIGHT fell suddenly in August 1943 at Son Krai in the heart of the Siamese jungle. The sleepy jungle bird noises, the delicate frou-frouing of the leaves of mighty trees, the busy sounds of hard manual work on the Burma railway, the 'railroad of death', suddenly switched off.

For a period of minutes only, there was a muting of sounds, a standing still of life, almost an expectancy. Lights, little fireflies of oil lamps began to cast a dull yellow gleam. The rows of attapp huts, bambooed and palm leaf thatched, loomed larger blacknesses against the uniform obscurity of the jungle. The night creatures came out and the good earth, a warm friend for the tired back, became a thing of menace, full of hidden dangers. The maddening 'tock-tock' bird began his cycle of tapping, the crickets, swollen with importance scraped and screeched with their hideous hindlegs and the bull-frogs chorus began.

In the hut at the foot of the hill a hundred men lay dying. A few, a very few of the last effects of cholera. Many with dysentery. All with the hint or certainty of malaria, tropical sores, and beri-beri, the dropsical vitamin deficiency disease.

I sat on the edge of the staging which constituted floor, furniture and bed, occasionally shifting position as the hard split bamboo of which it was made, obtruded too hardly on my thin shanks. I sweated profusely, slapped ineffectively at mosquitoes and ruminatively scratched where some particularly vicious insect decided that I tasted succulent. Yet I was no patient — I was Night Wardmaster. The years of training, my study and vocation, my experience in action, the Red Cross brassard which could not be worn because there was nothing to pin it to except seven and a bit stones of skin and bone, all these put me in charge of four medical orderlies for a period of twelve hours of darkness, having the care of one hundred sick and dying men.

Son Krai is probably covered by jungle now. There may be a vestige of the single track railway out there which crossed the wide river, or on the embankment where men were killed by falls of rubble. But what are a few deaths when the railway cost a death for each six feet of track? It existed then as a nightmare of smells, putrefaction, sweat, agony and hate. It was the second camp above Nieke where the cholera epidemic had seemed to start. Streams used for all purposes, Burmese higher up carrying the disease, Europeans crowded into impossible conditions, tired, emaciated, starving and brutally overworked. The alchemy of terror — terror from man and terror from disease. Half the men in camp died from it.

"Time for rounds," — the Corporal stood in front of me with his sheaf of bamboo tablets, lightly pencilled. We walked our macabre way the length of that suffering hut. Some were the lucky patients who slept, or seemed to sleep.

Here is one who cannot walk because the hole in his leg caused by a tropical ulcer has laid bare the bone for three inches of his shin. But the filthy lips of the wound are clouding over and closing in and they must not be allowed to do so until they are, if ever they are, pink and red and angry looking, and preferably bleeding freely with life in them for that is the only way to recovery. I leave an orderly with him, scalpel delicately scraping — the patient biting his blankets. There will be more like him and some will be quiet, and some will groan, and some will call in terror on their loved ones, and the orderly will hardly hear — his ears deafened by the hardness which mercifully lets him carry out his duty.

Now here is a man apparently sleeping peacefully, yet we know that only one hour ago his belly was racked with the draining purges of dysentery. He cannot be asleep. I pull back the blanket. His eyes are open. I feel his wrist. "Get him taken outside Corporal. Use a handkerchief for his face. Put his blanket in the tank. As quietly as you can."

A man rushes past me. He is fortunate. He only has to be in hospital in case he gets worse. At the moment he runs outside to the necessary place about twice an hour. He *could* recover.

A stream of mumbled and disjointed words comes to our ears. The man lies huddled under blankets — we had somehow found three for him. But his shivering seems to shake the very hut. His shoulders jerk, his teeth chatter, his skin is dry and cold, the blessed sweat he needs so badly is long in coming. This is no ordinary malaria such as most of us have more or less all the time, such as I have had for the last three days. This is a more malignant type. This turns a man mad, gives him delusions of grandeur, nerve racking nightmares and in the infrequent moments of awareness an overwhelming wish to die. We can do nothing for him.

Now here is someone for whom we have been able to do something. He had unbelievably an uncomplicated attack of appendicitus. He was operated on in the hut called the operating theatre, with the equipment called the surgical equipment, by the doctor called the surgeon, under the out of date anaesthetic. The unbelievable part is that he is still alive after twenty-four hours, and because he is, he has more than an even chance that he will live. I bet the Corporal a spoonful of rice that he will, but he shakes his head.

So we are at the end of one side and retrace our steps along the other. Two hours almost have passed in walking down, the hand of help, the little attention.

I come to the doorway and lean against the post looking up at the treetops and beyond them to the beautiful stars. I am no medical man — I was a kind of clerk before the world went mad. But I became a Territorial and the nearest unit was the R.A.M.C. I am a Warrant Officer. Here in Son Krai I am one of a few trying desperately to live up to a vocation, and doing anything by way of duties.

That was a calm and peaceful night so far as the jungle was concerned. The night creatures' noises had reached their usual level, not soft, not loud, but insistent — a background of the tropics. The treetops stirred so very slightly in a tiny breeze, a mere breath coming down from the higher hills to the north. The stars shone milkily in a sea of velvet indigo — the deep dark blue of the middle of the world. Even the mountain stream — a potential killer yet the only source of water, seemed to murmur caressingly over its pebbly bed.

"Midnight," said the Corporal. "Should be some tea." Magic promise but poor fulfilment. The dust the Japanese called tea and issued to us their captives, bore no resemblance to anything ever seen in tea cups or packets in a grocer's store. But it could be infused in boiling water and it was warm and gratifying, and somewhere in its smoky depths it carried a hint of Home. We drank it, sitting on the ground, the night air around us, and the ward of men behind us.

There was a burst of shouting. It came from the Japanese barrack hut up on the hill. It sounded like a drunken party — some festival, religious or otherwise. A handful of guards overseeing a thousand men. No need for barbed wire or barricades. Only a perfunctory picket mounting for where was there to run? Only hundreds of miles of almost impenetrable jungle and beyond that no friendly forces for perhaps a thousand miles. Saki the fermented rice wine, was a powerful drink. I remembered 'they' our captors, had given us some — was it last Christmas? About a cupful a man. Potent, fiery, liquid metal, it caught the breath, gripped the vitals and exploded in the brain like an injection of steam. I hoped they would keep their high spirits in their own compound and not decide upon some devilment to torment us.

I go back in the hut and start some office work. The light is a wick of flannel pushed through a tin lid into a tin filled with palm oil. Thick red and a little nourishing, it is also almost the only source of illuminant. It smells horribly. There is some paper, which must be jealously used and only for what are intended to be more permanent records. For the most part bamboo is used. Shaved or rubbed so that its convex face becomes flat it can be written on in pencil and washed off. It is ideal for patients' diagnoses and treatment records — the records are almost always short.

"Can you come?" A voice in the darkness which is the central aisle attracts my attention. It is an orderly. He looks afraid — no aware.

I get up. I ask. "What's up?"

"It's that beri-beri case — his breathing — I think he's going."

We go down to where he lies. Grossly bloated under his blankets, swollen with the water that comes from lack of vitamin B1, he has lain still and uncomplaining, quietly drowning in his own serum. Now he is gasping. His breath is laboured. I can feel no pulse in spite of digging my fingers into his inflated wrist.

"How long like this." I asked. The Corporal has come up.

"Last couple of hours — shall I get the M.O?"

A heavy decision — yet not so heavy for this is no unusual occurrence. To disturb the Medical Officer unnecessarily will be unkind. There are so few of them and they have so much to do between operations and treatments and keeping sickness in themselves at bay. If he comes, what can he do? There are no drugs to pull this man back from the grave. There are *none*. There are no injections to alleviate his symptoms. These must be saved for those more likely to benefit from them. What he needs is massive doses of the vitamin. The nearest is thousands of miles and a jungle away.

"No," I say. "It's a waste of time." I sit on the staging by the patient. "All right — I'll stay here." I say. I sit and look at this monstrous mountain that once was a virile man. If I had tears I could have shed them, but tears were squeezed dry many months ago. I wonder who he left behind when he came to this hostile land. Will there be those who mourn? Or will his passing when it finally is known be unremarked or rewarded with. "Oh really? Hard luck."

He seems to be trying to say something and I lean over him to catch the faintly whispered words. Each breath is an agony of effort. Ah! there I have it. He said — what foolishness is this — he said. "Bloody lovely dinner." I try to get through to his mind. I speak into his ear but there is no response. Steadily his breathing becomes worse. Quietly he dies. He is taken outside.

I have been with him for two hours. In that time the hut all around me has been murmurous. There have been sounds — the normal sounds of a hospital ward. Sounds that one gets used to and which only clamour for attention if they are extraordinary.

I go for a wash in the little stream now reasonably safe to use. One must be careful not to get the water into or on one's mouth but otherwise it is a clear stream. The air seems chilly. It is the small hours of the morning and the temperature has probably dropped to about seventy degrees. As I wash I get a mental picture of Home. I am back two years ago in the middle of manoeuvres in Staffordshire. It must have been spring or autumn — it was not warm enough for summer and yet the coldness of the water when I washed before climbing back into the lorry had not had the biting chill of winter. It also then was about two or three or four o'clock in the morning — that dead time when life seems at its lowest ebb. We were on some exercise or other which no doubt satisfied those who organised it of their astuteness and of the stupidity of unit commanders. We went nowhere special; we did nothing useful, but we were moved about in a gigantic chess game and thus were made ready for war.

I dried myself and went back into the hut. What else was there to do. What in fact *could* be done. There was noise at the far end. Another still form was being carried outside. That must be one of the advanced dysentery cases. I gather the staff together and we have a re-assessment of the situation. Almost this could be comical because there is nothing to re-assess. In fact it seems that the most urgent need, that is to say the most urgent capable of ever being satisfied, is for more bedpans. So a request must go to the 'carpenter's shop' for more of these to be made from the giant bamboos. I check the equipment we have. Two thermometers, two precious thermometers, a few simple instruments, a few home-made dressings.

One orderly starts some unpleasant laundering at the tank just away from the hut. Another cleans the instruments yet again. There is no protection for them and they rust in one humid night. Yet another goes around quietly 'tidying' where he can. I begin writing a brief report. The Corporal says. "Four o'clock." — he still has a watch which works. Mine only has the second hand, useful for pulses but hopeless for judging the passage of time. He goes to see if the early turn cooks have come on duty and could by chance be re-boiling the over-tired tea.

I have an attack of the miseries. We have had one batch of mail delivered to us. Each of us has received in varying degree a collection of letters sent to us covering a period of perhaps twelve months. There is no coherence about them for many are missing. The addresses from which they are written change. In one someone is sick. In another someone else's loss is referred to but it is not clear who or what has been lost. We have had the doubtful privilege of writing one stereotyped postcard. But after all it is only two years and two months since we became prisoners. We are the forgotten. The news we hear, mostly from the pirate radios we operate, suggests a great pre-occupation in England with the problems of the Hitler War. The Far East seems to have been forgotten. Do they know, we wonder, about the march, through seventeen nights from a village north of Bangkok to the camp in the jungle below the river? Do they know we carried what we could and jettisoned the rest? That we had only one meal by night and one by day and that the jungle path was often knee deep in mud and if you fell, you probably stayed there? Do they know what it feels like to have a rifle butt brought across your shoulders because you lag behind? No. They will never know.

The orderlies have finished their chores and are sitting talking quietly in a corner. The Corporal has come back with some tea. He tells me the latest rumours from the cookhouse — about as reliable as a prognosis on the patients but still diverting to discuss.

When we feel the night will never end there is a pause in the chorus of jungle sounds, a break, a hesitancy which by its very difference draws attention to itself. Within seconds it seems the tempo has changed; the pitch of the symphony of the night creatures has gone. Other sounds have taken their place. It must be dawn. The tops of the trees are now clear and sweeping in comes the day. The little oil lamps are put out. The sleeping men stir, for life is adjusted to the rise and fall of the sun.

Now we can make all tidy. Patients who are helpless can be given what passes for a wash. Those who can will crawl to the edge of the staging and be helped to wash in the bamboo bowls. There can be a scraping or sweeping of the dirt floor. The 'laundry' can be spread to dry. Breakfast — the bowl of white rice and the half cup of makeshift tea, slightly sweetened for those on the dangerously ill list, can be brought and dispensed. The pots have to be washed.

The orderlies, heavy-eyed come to report their tasks accomplished. Ordinary men, plumbers, clerks, miners, men from any walk of life faithfully, and without complaining, doing tasks which might turn the stomach of many a State Registered Nurse back in England. True to their Corps motto 'In Arduis Fidelis' — now to be translated 'Faithful in great hardship'.

The Corporal yawns. He tries a joke but it fails. My relief comes. I tell him what is to be told and go outside. As I walk back to my six feet of hut space higher up the hill I pass the long line, it is ten this morning, of those who found peace in the night. Stretched naked and unashamed, only their faces covered, they lie, mute testimony to the cruelty of man to man.

13 Out of the Jungle 1944

SO the diary goes on:

August 15th 1943 *"Eighteen months to the day and date of capitulation and I am lousy — actually lousy as most people are here. We have had another injection for Cholera and Plague."*

August 16th *"Stuart Livesley died this morning — [a damned shame because eventually despair forced him to stop fighting]."*

This was the second of those instances where it was demonstrated that health had little to do with living, and death only marginally to do with pathological conditions, but rather with the mind and will. Stuart Livesley was my friend — one I had made when at school in Varndean, Brighton. He was a year in front of me but we were members of various societies around the school and had much in common, including an inclination to learn other languages and in particular Spanish in one of our 'free' periods at school. He became expert in it and like me, but in Brighton, he joined the Territorial Army. He became a Corporal in the Intelligence Corps and before long was sent to the Far East. He too became a prisoner of the Japanese on 15th February 1942.

He went with 'F' Force to Thailand and I met him at Son Krai, for the second time, after a long time, when he was admitted to the hospital for dysentery. I had not even known he was in the camp. What a pleasure and a pain it was to see him and in the first two or three days as he recovered we spent hours talking over old times.

Then he was well again — at least as well as anyone could be and was due for discharge back to the coolie-like work of humping clay, and timber, and building the infamous railway. He said to me that he thought he would not 'go out' again with Them. He would, as the Australians called it 'bludge' — in other words shirk. He wanted only to 'lie in bed'. I pleaded with him to get up and go out. The M.O. was coarser in his comments and said Stuart had to leave the next morning; but when the next morning came he was even more listless and was running a high fever. There was no explanation for this. He had nothing clinically wrong with him. I spent the day pleading, arguing cajoling and threatening him — because I feared the truth of a saying and belief we had in the Medical Corps — 'If you want to die — just lie down'. The next day he was worse. Violent diarrhoea returned; his temperature fluctuated wildly, even his blood pressure and pulse dropped. The next morning he died — at 0855 hours — the 16th August 1943. He had simply given up — and died.

* * * * *

August 16th (continued) *"The name of this camp is Son Krai — but it's not as beautiful as it sounds. I am going ahead with my writing and am still optimistic."*

August 25th *"The Nips have decided we are no good at building railroads and have imported two thousand Burmese. It is very pleasant to see them working. More people have gone to Burma but the Nip insists that we are going back to Changi. In the meantime the monsoons are clearing up. Many ideas for new novels and a play but I have a fever, malaria and diarrhoea and do not feel like writing."*

September 3rd *"Moved hospital over to isolation. Very hard work lifting panniers and moving Nip nets. [From one side of river to other up the hill.]"*

September 17th *"My birthday. Four years wasted. Not quite, because I've been enabled to find my writing ability through being a prisoner. I have been unwell lately. Not really ill because I merely have occasional geri (diarrhoea) and headaches. Have had a row with one or two officers over my job and I think I came out on top because I am being treated better. The hospital is running smoothly and there is no more movement to Burma. The Nips have imported some Dutch of 'A' Force to complete the railway which should be here in a few days. Work on the road is almost at a standstill. Expecting Aussies from No. 1 camp and later to move further up, or back down to Malaya. Canteen supplies are reasonable and the food has improved a little. There is a possibility of Red Cross clothing coming in and we badly need them. We are in rags. The boot [this refers to Italy] is ours except for the shouting. It won't be long now.*

September 22nd *"Rumours still rife but no movement yet. Captain Watabiashi has gone to Burma. Canteen goods are trickling in and we have been issued with one pair of socks, grey cotton and wool, and one pair of shorts elastic white cotton both of very inferior quality to make up some of our clothing deficiencies. Most of us are literally in rags. The railroad was laid through here three days ago and trucks with lorries and engines [lorries* as *engines?] have been through. There is some movement of troops other than our force. We had a rat again last night. We are definitely going back to Changi. Birds [radios] have stopped singing and the weather is clearing up. We are digging slit trenches. I have scabies."*

October 16th *"I recovered from the diarrhoea but had a sequel in a pruritis on my fissure but most painful. Still no news of Changi. Cholera has started again in*

No. 3 camp [the camps were numbered downwards from the Burma end]. Our food isn't too bad now judged by Thailand standards. I am getting on with my play and have one or two fine ideas. After much patient waiting we have at last heard the birds singing but the song was disappointing [pirate radio news]".

October 18th *"Two days ago the first train (steam engine) went through here much to everyone's surprise for no one imagined that the banking would stand up to it. Rations are brown rice, watery stew for breakfast, white rice, bean stew or baked white for tiffin plus boxed yak stew, sometime sweet potatoes or even new potatoes for dinner. Haggy [Sergeant Hagmaier] and I have a better diet, however, by judicious use of canteen purchases i.e. small quantities of sago flour, oil, tinned fish, peanuts and by imaginative cooking on my part I have even made pasties and doughnuts. Wild pumpkin leaves grow here. We eat a lot of them. One sees domesticated elephants roaming in the jungle."*

October 31st *"Sunday. We have had a search today by the Nips. They descended upon us without warning and made a thorough search of all kit and medical panniers. They confiscated batteries, tools, soldering iron etc., and we sweated profusely."*

* * * * *

At the time our radio was contained in a biscuit tin and was operated by two R.A.M.C. Lieutenants — doctors both — and regrettably I have no note of their names. They operated in the 'officers' quarters a six foot by six foot space at one end to one side of the hut, opposite that occupied by myself as hospital manager and my dispenser Sergeant Hagmaier — referred to as 'Haggy'. The report came up the hill from the valley on the other side of the railway, where the 'working' men's camp was. Like jungle drums we knew the guards were on their way. There was a great deal of hiding of contraband but the radio was the thing. The Officer's head appeared above the screen they had with the tin in his hand. He handed the tin to me. "Lose it quick Q," he said. Now just how do you hide, in a matter of perhaps three minutes a tin of some prominence of colour, containing a radio, possession of which meant almost certain death of beheading by sword? The mind tends to seize up; the cogs do not move; there is a roaring in the ears.

I walked, somewhat quickly, down the centre of the hospital 'ward' between the two platforms of bamboo on which lay the patients; and out at the other end into the edge of the jungle — not more than five yards from the hut. This was secondary growth and light for about ten yards, having been cut back repeatedly. Walking steadily forward, with that uncanny hair-raising at the back of the neck, which comes with terror, not knowing if a Japanese soldier was one yard or fifty behind me, I pushed into the denser growth. I found what appeared to be an impenetrable bush and thrust the tin into it; turned, walked out, adjusting my G-string loin cloth and ragged shorts, in what must have been some of the worst ham acting ever.

The Japanese had reached the hospital. The first man had walked right through to station himself as some sort of guard at the end. He made an exclamation as I emerged from the scenery but as I bowed, and ostentatiously pulled my rags tigher around me, he obviously accepted that I had been into the jungle for personal hygiene, and let me go back into the hut.

Of course our latrines were in another direction; of course we would not normally go into the jungle indiscriminately to foul it; but the guard saw what he expected to see and I got back to my bedspace unmolested.

* * * * *

November 1st *"Monday. They returned them! Books were taken and later returned suitably marked. This [diary] and my others didn't go. [They took away our books and some which were little books that I had written whilst I was out there but were innocuous. Later, having decided there was nothing seditious in them, the Commanding Officer put his seal on them with Japanese writing to say it had been approved. So by simple transfer thereafter my diary even had the seal of approval on it]. The rumour about Changi is stronger now and today 4.11.43 we have had a cholera injection. I am reasonably healthy but have two to five stools in the night. I still have a little scabies but no lice. This place isn't very interesting although the weather is fine because there is no wild life or what there is doesn't come up to expectations."*

November 10th *"Held concert in ward on 5th. Good fun.*

'Three times a night,
three times a night,
see how we run,
see how we run,
we all sit out on the bog in a row,
cursing the War and the people we know,
we'll all be happy when we don't go
three times a night.'

The seal of approval

This is a photograph of the cover of the booklet referred to earlier in this book entitled 'Five Continents' which I allowed the guards to take away. Whoever inspected this and the novels and other books which were taken affixed a strip of paper with some light adhesive to the cover as seen below. Later I attached these strips to whichever of my books I wished to protect and used some form of [already used once] plaster. The signature was a red ink rubber stamp which is now indecipherable.

The Japan Information Centre at Grosvenor Square said in December 1982 that the transliteration is:

NIPPON-GUN KYO/KA ZUMI

and it means:

"With the Permission from the Japanese Army"

Further official camp concert on 7th at which Col. Dillon and Maj. Wilde performed to great reception. I have another go of diarrhoea but it is adequately fixed now. I have several septic spots on my feet. The rumours about Changi are stronger and look like fact. Arrangements have started for the move. I made some rice-polishing biscuits and some sweet potato cakes the other day. [Rice-polishings are the husks — very nutritious — but not a very pleasant taste. They are normally thrown away. The Japs wisely saved them]."

November 21st "*The move has started and one or two small parties have gone. Today we moved back again into the main camp. I seem to be very much persona grata with the Colonel.*"

November 23rd "*Moved from Son Krai by train at eight o'clock last night. Forty-five men to a truck including sick. De-trained at Nieke and were sorted. Heavy sick went on and I, Haggy and thirty-seven others were dropped off. Went to bed at four o'clock in bamboo rat infested Nip ration store. Looked like staying here the night at least. Met some of the 197; Keegan, Hellawell, Brown, Davison, Charge, and Page who are attending bhongs [the local jungle natives — an Australian word]*".

November 25th "*We were told to move at four o'clock on 23rd but were almost immediately dismissed. At eight o'clock while Haggy was out on a working party he alone was detailed to go and we said cheerio. Went to bed. Awakened at one thirty moving in half an hour. Met Percy (Haggy) who hadn't gone. Loaded onto trucks, forty-five men per open truck. Sat there in misery for four hours. Breakfast at six and haversack rations. Eventually moved at eight on 24th. Very smutty from engine. Passed some camps I recognised including Shimo Nieke. Long halt at Taranahouiphei where we caught up with Mr. Childs train from Burma twelve hours before us and where another Burma train came in. Moved about six and reached Praigui or Plankam [Hitler's old camp] at one in morning today. Had meal, slept on siding. Breakfast at eight o'clock. Bathed in river and very gratefully. Left after tiffin. About two o'clock all three trains joined and made good time 'til four when just after passing a derailed truck, one of ours jumped the line ran upright for twenty yards. Men inside not too shaken. Truck back on at about six. We moved off soon after and stayed in train until eight a.m. on 26.11.43 when we arrived at Canburi. Food is very plentiful. I was very lucky and found a place in the tents but many slept in the bush. There are good canteen facilities but no meat has made its appearance yet. Met Jim Innes. Bananas and eggs are purchasable; good night.*"

November 27th "*Buggered about all day. Took down our tent but put it up in the same place. Caught up with the panniers again. Long check parades here. F &*

H forces are mixed up but theoretically separate. One thousand of F Force are detailed for Singapore but haven't left yet."

November 28th *"Sunday. Hoping for a yasume* [rest]. *Had a fair rest. Learned that Capt. Clarkson was here and some of 197. Also that Corp. Gibbs had died. Rained hard all night."*

November 29th *"I have acute balanitis* [*A painful inflammation and swelling of the glans penis*] *and I think I must have a circumcision here if necessary. I also have three small ulcers."*

December 3rd *"I went to Bampong on a lorry in an attempt to obtain some medical stores. I was unsuccessful because the stores are buried beneath a pile of officers' personal kit. Had a heavy day shifting boxes and uncomfortable journey in the lorry."*

December 6th *"Had a fever like the Son Krai one but feel a little better today. We moved again yesterday to a leaky tent and as there has been a considerable amount of rain are not very happy. Haggy and I are still together but a lot of medicals have already gone up to the hospital. We are anxious to go. Water is the biggest problem in this camp. I have bought a clarinet for $10 — approximately 5s. It is not in very good condition but is repairable."*

December 5th *"Recovering from my sickness and doing very little work. Not anxious to go to the hospital unless it rains."*

December 9th *"Moved down to hospital camp and went straight away into diet kitchen I am to run. I should get fit here. Had poor night because it was so cold. Am steadily mending my clarinet."*

December 10th *"The hospital camp is a good place. A view of the* [*railway*] *line and a decent scene; well laid camp. Plenty of good food. I live and work in the ration store of the diet kitchen where food is extra good. Mr. Sindon was with us but movement down to Singapore started. The kit camp evacuated and Mr. Sindon went along and the camp is reduced to a bare minimum of very sick and staff who expect to stay in Thailand for two months. We are moving to the 'fit' camp in two days. One can get a girl for $1 50 through the fence. Afraid I am not interested. Capt. Clarkson is here and have been very pleased to meet him again."*

* * * * *

Captain Clarkson had been the Dental Officer attached to the 197 Field Ambulance and I was with him on the Empress of Asia when she was set afire in the Straits before Singapore. We occasionally met later in the course of duties but to meet him here again was a distinct pleasure. I offered to help him in his dental surgery and he was glad of the assistance — no one really fancied the job as there was little anaesthetic and instruments were either primitive or worn out or both.

However a stream of men came through the bamboo box we called the surgery, after having waited in the bigger bamboo box designated the waiting room, and passing the registering Corporal in what might have been termed 'reception'. Old men, and young, English, Australian, Anglo-Indian, Hindu, Parsee and the occasional Japanese or Korean.

I watched, and helped, fascinated as the foot-operated drill bored out the inside of molars and marvelled at the relatively large cavity it made. On one occasion, when a nerve had to be killed, Capt. Clarkson put a 'gunge' (as a temporary filling) into the cavity and sealed it with what I believe was gutta percha. I understand that too hot food or drink could dissolve the covering and the 'gunge' would then be swallowed with the food. It occurred to me that the insertion of a gunge made up with violently infective dysentery bacilli with only a light covering could effectively be a weapon for disposing of an enemy. I said so, and the Captain agreed — with the theory.

Later I wrote another novel, another detective story, in which this was the method of murder used (although cyanide was substituted for dysentery) so that when 'Feloniously and Wilfully' by Ernest Wood (my pen name) was published in 1947 I could claim the method and plot was original in this respect. There is no copyright in ideas and the method has been used by others since then.

December 20th *"Little sleep last night owing to outside circumstances [air raids]. My balanitis continues and my fissure has erupted but otherwise I am reasonably happy. [How extraordinary this reads!]."*

January 1st 1944 *"First day of New Year. Have had a varied fortnight. On the 21st I had an operation under chloroform and ether to repair an anal fissure — by Col. Houston. On 23rd I was shifted with the rest of the camp back to the original 'fit' camp. On 24th I had a touch of cerebral malaria and had an intravenous quinine. [The disease must have upset my calculation of the dates. It could not have been on the date the diary says — not physically possible.] Christmas Day menu breakfast: rice porridge, egg and chips. Lunch: roast duck and roast potatoes, roast papaya and plain cake pudding. Tea: shepherds pie. I was discharged from hospital on 27th and owing to the closing of the diet kitchen put in charge of the library and lectures."*

* * * * *

A word of explanation is necessary of the apparently sumptuous repast noted above. Special occasions like Christmas were marked by special meals contrived by hoarding a little of anything 'extra' that came in until it was needed. This reduced normal rations by small amounts from time to time — except in the hospital for the patients. Potatoes would have been sweet potatoes, all flour would be from sago; meat would be offal and rubbish cooked to distraction and minced; the reference to roast duck amazes me. This was one of the best fed camps because of the proximity of Thai villages.

* * * * *

January 12th *"The other day I went to Bampong collecting attapp. A pleasant change after being in camp. We heard about damage lower down. Had to work with Thai girls who were very friendly. Camp is getting better each day as we are improving the cooking and sanitary conditions and building huts. There are no rumours about moving. Not yet been able to mend my clarinet. My rear is very comfortable. We have had the 'mango' rains and I didn't get too damp."*

February 2nd *"Time passes very quickly. I have had fever and diarrhoea and felt low until a scorpion stung me [after which I felt better!] We had an anti-rat day yesterday because a rat in Kanchanabri village died of plague (?) Also we have seen fleas. The W.Os now live in a hut which is of course bug infested. I am giving the 196 a hand with their magazine. Rumours are good. Capt. Watabiashi has gone to Burma [again] and we expect the Tanbaya crowd any day."*

February 19th *"Although I don't write this up every day the days are full of incident [which would be interesting] to people at home. The magazine is not yet finished — this is typical of the 196. I am hoping to produce my own play here. For the last week I have been running a supper bar on the Changi lines but there is of course the usual foolish opposition. Tambaya has been evacuated here and we have to put up with [............] and others. Rumours are plentiful. Some passed on by the Thais. The Japanese are digging themselves trenches and certainly it would appear that they are necessary. I don't sleep too well but that doesn't matter. Pretty well apart from some diarrhoea."*

March 3rd *"I have had a bout of BT + + malaria. Very uncomfortable. My tail end has also given trouble. I have an ulcer on my foot. All these ulcers leave semi-permanent brown marks. The snack bar has been discontinued as a punishment for demonstration on parade. This was caused by the Court Martial and public flogging of Private Dixon [not the real name] for theft and illegal sales.*

* * * * *

Manners, moral, crime and even sin, change with the times, and what was an unmannerly, amoral crime and deadly sin a hundred, or even a few years ago may today be at least tolerated, if not accepted or possible even approved. If you doubt me think about children born out of wedlock, or rather their parents, and homosexuals. There is nothing to guide in this matter of right and wrong except what is current at the time.

Accordingly wrong doing in the army has a different meaning from wrong doing in civvy street; and what was a crime in the services bore no resemblance to the standards we had as prisoners in these extreme circumstances.

Many things were excused for the sake of maintaining the rest of discipline and control through the tenuous network of sergeants and corporals, so that the Officer in charge of the troops could present a bland face to the Japanese overlords.

The biggest crime, or one of the worst, was theft from one's fellows: 'Winning' things elsewhere, even trading 'over the wire', sometimes had justification but to steal from one's mates was hideous.

This Private Dixon had done just that, and in addition (for we never knew all the details) probably had stolen something and tried to sell it to the Japanese. There was a properly constituted Court Martial and a verdict of 'Guilty' found. The worst punishment which it was possible to inflict in these circumstances it seemed, was a public flogging.

All fit troops were paraded on thc large parade ground in a hollow square. Private Dixon was bent over a table and some [perhaps a dozen] strokes of the cane were inflicted on his rump. Humiliating for him but no doubt effective. Unfortunately many of the troops had no idea what it was all about and objected to such humiliation being brought upon one of our own in sight of the Japanese. Thus there was a demonstration which could have turned into a near riot. Swift action stopped it however, and the parade was dismissed but the C.O. decided the whole camp needed to learn a disciplinary lesson and cut off one of the few 'pleasures' then available.

* * * * *

March 5th *"The nights are very quiet now and I sleep better. The magazine is finished but the play hasn't progressed much."*

EVENTIDE

When evening comes and light begins to fade,
The tree tops whisper; green hills turn to blue,
Then let your thoughts go with the setting sun,
To lands that speak of home and kindred too.
When day is done, the hurly-burly stilled,
And petty piques have no more power of pain,
Then still your fears, forget your nagging care,
And let unbounded optimism reign.
When o'er the boundless dome of azure sky,
The shadow creeps and deep blue stillness comes,
Then picture far off armies brave and free,
And thrill to hear the loud victorious drum.

For eventide is when our caged wills,
Are free to soar away above the hills.
21.1.44

March 28th *"Because daily life is almost without incident, I have neglected to write this up. K & L forces left us on 26th, including Capt. Clarkson. They have gone up the road a little way. 'A' force is still in Thailand much to everybody's surprise. We have had a search by the guards. My books were untouched. [Because of the 'approval' sign]. The snack bar opened again almost immediately and I am still in business. [Profits went to a Welfare Fund]. We think we shall go down in about a fortnight. WO 2 Dave Wharton has offered me a job in Australia; wages and commission and living expenses — about £12 a week. I have provisionally accepted and drawn up an agreement. I have written three short stories and a book on Judo for Dave and I have scrapped the idea of putting on a play as one receives no co-operation unless one is of the elite [refers to some members of the 196 Field Ambulance].*

On April 1st I went down with fever, the second bout of malaria in one month. It makes one very weak and depressed and spineless. I also have a broken rib now nearly mended. We had the first concert and a mock trial down here the other day. We hear from Capt. Clarkson that the Tamils at his camp are dying of thirst. We are for glass rodding on the 6th which suggests an early move. The sky is still worth noticing."

* * * * *

Undoubtedly these cryptic comments about 'the sky' or 'quiet nights' refer to the flying over of allied planes. Whilst my books had received the seal of approval it was still undesirable to be too explicit in case an inquisitive English reading Japanese Officer chose to pry.

Glass rodding referred to the annoying habit the Japanese had of regularly so-called testing us for dysentery. This was achieved by parading all Officers and other ranks before two or three [imaginary] medical orderlies who had been detailed for the job by their Gunso Sergeant Major only a short while before. In the beginning the instruments used were cylindrical glass rods, about six inches long and perhaps 3/8th of an inch in diameter, ground smooth, and inserted with a little care into the anus of the soldier patient bent over before the 'medical orderly'.

We all thought this hilarious in one respect as we were undoubtedly bowing before the 'master' race, but presenting them with an appropriate portion of our anatomy. However the joke wore thin when the orderlies lost patience and became less careful about the insertion and when later the supply of glass rods ran out and there were substituted some very coarsely sanded bamboo rods on which to obtain specimens.

Some paid others to take their turn — I was one because the operation had left that part of my rear extremely uncomfortable and tender. It was rumoured that there were one or two who were actually happy to go round the second time — but each to his liking!

* * * * *

April 5th *"We are to be moved to Singapore. Bum prodding on the 7th. I fear a sea trip under the Nips. We all do. I have an idea not for the first time to write a book about myself and opinions possibly to be entitled '30'. I have many writing commitments. Some of my short stories and both novels have been read aloud in the wards."*

April 20th *"It appears as though the move has temporarily fallen through. Money is very short because we spent in anticipation of the move yesterday. I had to write an appreciation of Thailand which the Col. wants for the Kempitai (Military Police). The only subjects about which we could write were climate, country, people and customs. The weather is cooler now and starting to break up. Padre Cordingley [an R.C. Padre] and Pat Woolfe [an Anglo-Indian Medical Officer] were given two days handcuffs for communicating with outside camp."*

14 Return to Singapore

MAY 2nd 1944 *"We left Canburi on 22nd. The journey took five days. There were eight meal points. Twenty-five men to a truck including six stretcher cases. Found conditions were changed from the journey up. Thai Tickals worth two Malayan dollars. Arrived in Singapore at six a.m. on 28th, one year and four days after leaving. Acted as loading party so stayed in Singapore a little longer. Rode in lorries. Very nice to see such a large town again and the place looks far happier than the towns in the countries further north. Went to Selarang where everybody is very pleased to be back to the outward signs of civilisation. Showers, stone buildings etc. Had a good welcome from the 197 chaps."*

May 4th *"There is a move in the air and some separation and segregation is indicated. We are not wanted much by the HP [hospital people] and are being pushed around by our own F Force people. Saw a splendid show 'Suspect'. Had a drink with Henry in fairly reasonable quarters. They have docked us more than 50% of our April pay. We hear there is some Red Cross stuff about."*

May 5th *"Had a bum prod yesterday. Eddy Entwhistle one of my storemen in the 197 went for operation on a whitlow and was given a general [anaesthetic] because there is no local. He passed into a coma and died about ten o'clock in the morning. One more death due to carelessness."*

May 10th *"Buried Eddy on the 5th. Saw AIF review and have heard some new recordings on the electric gramophone. Received 1/7th of a Red Cross parcel — American. Several letters. Sent our third card home yesterday. I have two large boils. I believe I am going with the 197 when we move."*

May 31st *"A lot has happened in three weeks. On 19th I went as one of the advance party to Woodland Camp Karanji to prepare for the hospital. A hutted camp but much better than anything up country. We had to work very hard but rations; rice, meat, tapioca root, were plentiful though poor quality. I had to screen — [put a fence of hessian round the camp] — for the guards with forty men. Water is laid to stand pipes. Back to bore-hole latrines again. Light from a diesel engine. Main hospital moved on 28th and 29th. One thousand and four hundred of them. Quite a lot of bludgers [shirkers — Australian word]. Very hard work unloading lorries, carrying wood etc. I sleep in a bunk, one of the best in the camp, which says very little with Chappy and J.J. Porter, the American saxophonist. I am on general* *duties which means I do anything at the beck and call of all seniors. I am not pleased with it. I feel pretty well, apart from some boils and tinea.* [*skin rotting*]*."*

June 8th *"I have been put to work on the IJA gardens which are not very productive, as Chappy is sick. I expect to be working full time in the Theatre soon and have had two more boils but otherwise OK."*

* * * * *

I appreciated the respect some Japanese had for death, when I was in charge of the burial parties. The first time we had a death in the camp, I was asked by Captain Yoshikawa who was in charge of the camp, to choose somewhere as a burial ground for this particular camp. It could be outside the wire, it did not matter, and so I went with the burial party and guard, and strolled up the hill. At the top of the hill I could see across the straits of Johore. I could see Palau Lubin, the little island to the North East of Singapore and thought this would be a good place to come, probably once a day, because I should have to perform this duty once a day at least. Needless to say, when I related my experience, someone of senior rank decided to take on the duty. I am very happy to say, that by a pure fluke the Imperial War Graves Commission, when hostilities ceased, decided that that cemetery site at Karanji should be one of the sites of official War Grave Cemeteries after the War. I haven't seen it since but I would love to now.

June 27th *"Tobacco is very short indeed. We are smoking papaya leaves. We have had a big row with the administration over the deductions in our Nip pay. One lot of patients have been received from Changi. I have had an attack of fever with acute diarrhoea but begin to feel better. Have lost weight steadily. I now weigh seven stone and eight pounds. Also I have shrunk one and quarter inches. Hope to get back home soon or there will not be many of us left. A lot of 'overland' men seem to have been drowned! Rations are now; rice, sugar, salt, tapioca root, palm oil, dried fish — about two ounces per month. I have been employed on erecting the inner barbed wire fence for the camp but am off duty now. Feel very sick and downcast. The War is nearly five years old. No news of the theatre job. Look like being an odd-job man after being up-country too! I wonder what makes us still want to live."*

July 11th *"Discovered I had worms* [*Ascarius*]*. Coughed one up about seven inches long. Had treatment, feel a little better now. On theatre staff. Gardens in morning and ward shows afternoons. Tobacco situation easier. Finished writing* [*book*] *'Merely Players' about pre-historic man. Plenty of ideas for more."*

July 26th *"Feel a lot better nowadays. In fair communication with Changi and been in correspondence with them. Had some more letters. Have started on the third detective novel which doesn't run at the moment.* [*This was the one subsequently published as 'Feloniously and Wilfully'*]. *Still work on company gardens in the morning. Theatre work, ward shows in the afternoon. Find our mental ability very poor and of course physical ability. All the money they pay us has to go in smokes. How we wish for a Red Cross ship."*

August 8th *"Had malaria, must be about thirteenth time. Continual diarrhoea. Food is still poor and we are losing lots of weight. There are more rackets here than there ever were in Chicago and police and officers are the biggest offenders. Things show no signs of improving here. In the Nippon Times we see disturbing reports of flying bombs. Makes one very anxious."*

August 17th *"TAB shot today. The greatest week of the decade.* [*Refers to allied bombing raids*]. *Putting on a little weight again. Now eight stone and nine pounds. Raid alarm two nights ago."*

August 31st *"This is the strangest POW camp ever. Some of the walkers in the wire* [*Japs*] *refuse to salute."*

September 17th *"My birthday and don't think I can possibly spend another one here. I am sick again. It seems to be a sort of general debility, low blood pressure, anaemia, loss of weight and now weigh eight stone."*

September 28th *"I had a sigmoidoscopy* [*a robust metal tube with a light and mirror at one end inserted into the rectum to examine parts of the intestine*] *yesterday, because I have had a lot of diarrhoea and a continual headache for fourteen days. No test is positive, however, so no-one knows what is wrong with me. We may no longer even write to Changi and only three exchanges of patients are permitted. The population seem to be leaving Singapore. Much traffic on the road which runs just outside. Played some chess. Having to do a lot of mending. Clothes are a real problem. They even sell IJA issued tobacco cured in horse urine through the canteen. Have heard we have a British Army rise of 10s. 6d. per week after five years service."*

October 5th *"I have BT + + Malaria and jaundice."*

* * * * *

THE THOUSAND DAYS
(11th October 1944)

Tomorrow and tomorrow,
The rolling vista of unending days
Unfolds before me.

A thousand dawns have seen us
Captive here.
Rain and sun, wind and warmth
  in long monotony,
  that palls.
As the days have been,
So they ever shall be.
World without end,
Captivity without end.
For this is my life, there has been no other.

There never was a world
  of fuss and bother
  over precious things.
Always there has been this meanly,
  petty and unlovely,
  futile and pointless grind,
Amongst the things uncleanly
  that live, and grow,
  and menace the sanity,
Of the mind.

Dawn comes creeping in,
  Soft-footed, tenuous, a thief,
Of the hours of darkness.
  The crepuscule is brief
Before the light begins.
The trees are strange,
  bamboo, rubber, palms,
  none of them calms
The torment of the walking mind
  Which shows a world,
Strange, unkind,
Even after a thousand days.

But the quiet of the dawn is short,
For the hateful life starts
  hurrying, scurrying, rushing and flurrying.
Undignified scamper to work
To 'carry out those duties'
That 'have been assigned.'

To finish them, few though they be,
  for few work hard.
There's the rattle and clatter of typewriters,
The popping profusion of the engine,
Hard hammering, the scrunch of trailers.
All form a garland of hated work,
  for a hated people.
A garland around the busy oases
  of the wards
Where some lie dying and some lie sick,
And some lie battening
Like the bloated tick,
Sucking, fattening,
Not working but keeping away,
From anything that pulls them down.

"I must get home — why think of others,
"I call no men brothers —
"Let them die — not I"

But a few are making,
  an effort of will,
And some are taken,
  over the hill,
And the bugle, (otherwise forbidden) shrieks out.

Tiffin is past and the tempo slackens,
For all save the unfortunate rest.
If it rains, then bed is best
For the weather is chill,
To those who've been ill,
  and to those who haven't,
Their blood is thin,
And the cold creeps in.
The heat too. The sun is hot,
Beating down on the pitiful plot,
Where plants are raised,
To supplement the food.

Drowsiness settles.
Some sleep, some read, some scheme,
Some talk, or think, or dream;
For a space each brain,
Can have freedom again.
  There is indifference.

The evening's the time,
When emotions climb,
  For each is free (comic word!)
  Strange things are heard.
A church service perhaps.
  (but a futile waste of time is this,
  for the ministers are worst
  criminals in this place)

Or a show, where,
Strutting upon a stage
Some evince strange civilised feelings,
  trying to recapture,
  the wild rapture
Of a period when — but No!
There never was such a time.
Others watch and listen,
  blase, same actors, same audience,
And at the back of the mind always the thought
  'How long Oh Lord — How long?'
Here is a gambling school:
In the painted imagery of cards.
  Some talk. (God! How they talk!)
There is a 'school' — some other game.
Heads together whisper of petty crime,
  how something can be got for nothing.

There is a bed (so called) made up for the night.
It's occupant strives to die in sleep
  for a while, and wake to a better day.
Light fails — the engine roars and thunders.
And only dim shapes can be seen.
Each globe masked and hidden;
Beneath a circle of light,
  around,
  the brown,
  of masking paper.

A flicker of the light,
   and night must fall.
Slowly the silence descends, and perhaps the moon,
   shines over all.

Threading through all there's a mad refrain
The things I hear again and again;
   the babble of tongues,
   Lagis, Bludger, Racket, Ferfie,
   Benjo, Black Market, Boreholes, Griff,
and the rest.
The continual quarrel between the nations.
Aussi v. Pommie, not to mention the Yanks and the Dutch.
Grumbling about the food,
   the money, the canteen,
Most of it justified and,
   "When are we going to get out?"

The sound of bugle calls,
   foreign to the ear.
The relentless life that goes on,
   'Outside the Wire'.
Food that palls,
   No seasons to the year.
The insect life, workings of the colon,
   In the cookhouse a fire.

A click and shout,
   the guard turns out,
And down the road,
   continual goad.
One walking by,
   I stand quite still,
No sound, no cry.
   I've had my fill.

Tomorrow and tomorrow,
Time rushes on;
It seems as though this sorrow,
Will not be gone.
I live in a world
That really lives;
The future unfurled,
No promise gives,
   Of better times.

This is real,
  I have known nothing else,
Sometimes I feel
  That what has been
For a thousand days,
  Will ever be;
With fearful gaze,
  I only see —
Tomorrow — and — tomorrow.

October 19th *"Feel much better. Still have jaundice. We have had several serious ARP rehearsals."*

October 28th *"Slowly recovering from jaundice. Have had beri-beri and balanitis, now a touch of diarrhoea. The show is on at the moment and I help backstage. We have had three air-raid alerts."*

November 2nd *"Finished my third detective novel 'With Malice Aforethought' [later titled 'Feloniously and Wilfully']. The fourth book in all. Still off duty with jaundice. We have a permanent brown out now. [This was something less than a black-out]."*

November 5th *"When my jaundice is cleared up, I have to go in hospital with hook worm. Had daylight raid fifty-one Fortresses today. No bombs dropped. Hungry all the time."*

November 18th *"Came out of hospital after treatment [Carbon Tetrachloride Icc] for hookworm. Raid warning this morning but no activity. Still thin eight stone. Having cat for dinner. [During our captivity we ate dog, cat, rat, and snake — all of them delicious when protein starved]. Have written ecclesiastical type book about up-country and poem re camp."*

* * * * *

DRAT THE ANOPHELES!

There's a buzzing around,
And you don't feel too sound,
And you creep to your bed very slowly;
In the small hours of morn'
Then you wish you weren't born,
For you wake and you are melancholy:

You're a horrible sight,
And it just serves you right,
To allow the predatory 'skeeter',
To have bitten you where,
You were carelessly bare;
And her wings not your hands were much fleeter.

When you try to sit up,
And you sigh for a cup,
Of some very strong, black and sweet coffee,
But there's none to be had,
And you feel very bad,
And you couldn't get dressed up for toffee.

Then your pulse rate they take,
And they ask where you ache,
And you tell them it's all body over,
And the pain in your head,
Makes you wish you were dead,
Then you shiver and don a pullover.

For the shivering starts,
In your nethermost parts,
And it covers you over in pimples,
As you shiver and shake,
You make the bed quake
And you yell out for herbs and for simples.

They then give you quinine,
With a taste that's obscene,
But your temperature only mounts higher;
Take a blood slide or two,
And the rugs cover you,
And you quickly begin to perspire.

When it's over and done,
And you've really begun,
To be feeling a little bit brighter,
When the medicine you've had,
Only makes you feel bad,
And your head gets a little bit lighter.

For you're dizzy and sick,
And your back's got a crick,
And you wonder if you will recover;
There are bells in your ears,
There are new unknown fears,
That your mind just begins to discover.

But when you've made your will,
Just because you're so ill,
And your abrupt demise you are fearing,
Then the ache and the pain,
That you've learned to disdain,
Just annoy you and start disappearing.

And when you've convalesced,
You will swear with the best,
That all over a very large area,
You will murder on sight,
All mosquitoes that bite,
And so never again get malaria!

2.12.44

* * * * *

December 3rd *"Conditions as before, very depressed. Just contracted BT + + malaria again. It's getting a habit. Written several poems. Have written scheme for murder story re a homicidal maniac but not enough paper to type it here I'm afraid. I am hoping to make an anthology of extracts from Shakespeare."*

Karanji Creek, from No. 3 hut, Karanji Hospital 29.9.44
Coloured crayon drawing by the author.

December 17th *"Little to record. Very near Christmas which will be a lean one. Am discharged to duty but no work found for me yet. Have typewriter of my own now but doing little writing. Few poems. Have promise of some paper for typing. Play mahjong fairly often. Learning Dutch. This is a good opportunity I should have taken before. First rectal holiday for eighteen months but very hungry. Am in rags. Have papayas [pawpaw] on one of my trees. [Typewriters were available because there was little paper or record keeping]."*

December 28th *"Christmas over and pleased. Had good day general yasume. Slightly more food than usual of everday items. One or two drinks of 'hooch'. Many drunk. Three bad sleepless nights owing to noise, diatic diarrhoea etc. On 26th put to work again after three months. Making a padang for a Nip parade ground. Should finish two days from now."*

15 The End in Sight 1945

TO SUSSEX

O give me my native Downs,
Softer than emerald hue;
With gentle white clouds a' crowning them,
Drifting across the blue,
  Where the air is sweet,
  And the grass is neat,
And soft to the feet with dew.

Then show me the rolling hills,
Mantled in golden gorse,
From Weald to the sea they sweep their way,
Showing their ancient force.
  And their lines are clean,
  And the best that's been,
To all who have seen their course.

The villages stand beneath,
Trees from a bygone day.
The fields in their glory spread around,
'Circled by flow'ring may.
  And the grass is lush,
  And the swaying rush,
Make peaceful the hush of day.

There are all the well-loved names;
Clanctonbury Ring, and Glynde;
The Wilmington Man deep cut in chalk,
Arundel stands behind.
  Beachy Head and Hurst',
  Devil's Dyke where first,
Old Satan, accursed, had mined.

Thus cradled 'tween sea and sky,
Hills ever watchful stand,
With rolling green arms of softness sublime
Prof'ring a helping hand.
  And the wanderer may,
  Though he be far away,
See clearly his native land.

And could I but tread again,
Soil that is chalk and loam;
Where folks are all fair and free as the wind,
Peaceful by hills of home;
  Then I would abide
  Where the Downs kiss the tide,
And never decide to roam.
2.12.44.

January 9th 1945 *"Found wood-ash water takes oil out of clothes. Still writing a little. Have the feeling that madness is the only escape. Feel very overwrought. Play bridge in the evenings now."*

January 10th *"Heavy bombing raid. One bomber brought down. Pieces of engine [instruction] book [?] came floating down."*

February 2nd *"One hundred supers [fortresses] over yesterday. Lots of bombs dropped. Much shrapnel in camp. One piece landed on my bed. Two hours raid. This is my 7th day of malaria. Have had bad time this time. Two ounces fresh fish per man yesterday. First for very long time. Getting no protein."*

February 7th *"Just recovered from violent colic lasting thirty-six hours with no sleep. Feel better now. A lot of it in camp. Small amount diarrhoea. Craze for cowering in trenches. No good. Almost everyone has a trench now. A guard beat up a man yesterday for failing to give proper respect. We are optimistic, however. Have nearly completed a work of excerpts from Shakespeare. Rations are worse than ever. Almost no dried fish."*

February 13th *"Yesterday two prisoners who were in for trading in drugs were sentenced to periods in the Nip boob [jail]. The Chinese boy involved was freed and the escaped prisoner, a mental patient, missing for four days was recaptured two miles away and brought in. It is difficult to convince 'them' that he is mental. We have recce planes almost every day but not always a warning. Rations have been cut throughout the island. We now have 400 grammes of rice per day, very few veg. or anything else. Everyone hungry. Fortunately smoking takes away some of the hunger. Do a fair bit of gardening in my own garden. Made curry yesterday."*

February 15th *"Three years today became prisoner. Feeling exceptionally well. Rations now 400 grammes rice, 2 ozs. veg. ¼ oz. fish, ¼ oz. salt, 1 oz. oil, ⅛ oz. sugar per day. Have recce planes almost every day. Very hungry. Great shortage of paper. Have completed Shakespeare book."*

March 10th *"Rice reduced to 290 grammes per day. Total food eaten in one day now weighs 1 lb. We are smoking papaya and tobacco stalks. Am hoping to put my play 'Peculiar Prodigal' on here."*

March 24th *"Rice dropped 55 grammes in favour of maize. Everybody very hungry. Some are eating rats, snails and frogs. Manage to get some greens off my garden every day. Am feeling remarkably well. Weigh less than eight stone. We think Changi jail will be broken up to Singapore and we are to get over six hundred patients which means we shall be much more crowded than we are now. Things are rapidly becoming much more unbearable. We hope it will not be for long. We may have to lose the theatre. We have not heard any more of the Red Cross ship. I could scream for things like bread and cheese, bully beef or tea with milk."*

April 2nd *"Very eventful week. Had our first serious night raid. Three medical groups detailed to operate with working parties on defenses. Thirteen huts of camp wired off. Taken over by working party. Much movement in camp. Most of group personnel living in theatre. I on stage, packed and waiting for three days so far. Work party in this camp already received some Red Cross stuff. Lost my garden when we moved of course. Tension high, expectancy good. Feel fit but hungry all the time. Sleeping well. New pair of clogs made. Very wet weather."*

April 17th *"Medical Corps finally started moving on 12th. We went over wire into old camp. Very crowded quarters sleeping on floor. My plank bed stolen. Food fairly good about half as much again as in the hospital area. The working parties bring in large quantities of food. Major Bull, the OC, did not arrive until today. Reasonable treatment and agreement between personnel until today. Quarrel over the Red Cross pay and RAMC rations. Have had oatmeal and marmalade in small quantities. Row over ranks and I have made a complaint against the Adjutant for a remark passed by him. [I have no idea what this is about this long time after the event.]"*

May 12th *"In this camp one month. Things running smoothly now. Rations unchanged. I have had ascaris again but am better now. We shall not forget early morning of the 8th in a hurry. We had the biggest and closest thunderstorm I've ever been in. The wire surrounding the camp was struck otherwise the month has been very quiet."*

May 22nd *"Recurrence of ascaris admitted to ward for few days. Discharged today. Received tri-chlorethylene treatment which is unpleasant and dangerous. Also sulphaguanadine to stop vicious diarrhoea. Feel weak but OK. Have regained interest in note-making for books Inspection by General Shaito. 1192 days."*

May 26th *"Red Cross stores received in very bad condition. Some to be issued tonight. Very small quantities of course. Nips have also issued one towel (sweat rag) one piece of soap, one G-string each. Also some 'passion pants' all very poor quality of course. Very hungry no tobacco. Poor cheroots and stalks only."*

June 2nd *"Yesterday a Nip and a POW were killed in a fall of earth in one of the tunnels due to insufficient precautions having been taken. This is not the first death of this kind. Still having very small items of Red Cross supplies."*

June 26th *"A week ago 335 additional men were sent into the camp. They do not share our Red Cross rations. Only two more huts given us so now seventy sleep in a hut and many underneath. Have had two major operations in our gimcrack theatre but reasonably successful."*

* * * * *

This was the beginning of a series of major operations carried out in the most horrifyingly primitive conditions. The diet at this time consisted mostly of rice which was so contaminated with rubbish that it could not be washed completely clean. Rat droppings and grit were present in considerable quantities. Perhaps this, with general malnutrition was a contributory cause to the very large incidence of perforated gastric or duodenal ulcers. What would happen is that if the sufferer were fortunate his collapse occurred in the camp or if out on a working party the Japanese allowed him to be brought into camp. Less lucky ones had to wait until the main party returned from work.

In either case the risks patients ran were enormous, and the skill of medical officers and Medical Corps orderlies just short of miraculous. The operating theatre was simply a portion of one hut formed into a 'room' with requisitioned mosquito nets. Sterilisation of the area was by antiseptic spray and could only be minimal. Operating table was constructed of bamboo of course with boiled blankets as a sterilised cover. Surgical instruments, apart from a few genuine articles rapidly wearing out, were contrived out of army issue knives and imaginative use of all kinds of materials. Anaesthetic was often 'primitive' in the sense that it consisted of methods used fifty years before, and/or of materials long 'out of date', such as chloroform.

The patient was borne into the theatre after some attempt at cleansing his body and shaving the area of incision. M.Os and orderlies did what they could to make themselves sterile, and boiled and re-used rags became bandages. The operation proceeded under the meagre one or two light bulbs allowed us by the Japanese. Most operations had to be done in the evenings after dark because it got dark by eight o'clock and the men often did not come back until six. Moreover the guards would often cut off the electricity supply at 'lights out' ten o'clock. However I had organised so that if this happened we repeated the process first done in Singapore three years before of a procession of highly unsterile orderlies entering the 'theatre' bearing our home made lamps of wicks in oil.

Still there are many men walking about today who passed safely through these risks.

* * * * *

June 26th (continued) *"Have improvised concerts on yasume days. Remainder of Red Cross received in camp. Issued with three Nip cigarettes per day. Things very quiet. Am kept busy with RSMing and Q and the dispensing for this place. Have about sixty patients. Slit trenches under huts. Nips have given us a little more cooking equipment."*

July 17th *"Red Cross rations nearly finished. Learning a little Malay. Have ascaris again but no efficient treatment so grin and bear it. Some diarrhoea. Fell off veranda! Think I've cracked my wrist. Nearly healed now. Big rumours of moves. Had my kit searched. Prices ridiculous. Things very quiet. Padre Chambers died of pancreatitis."*

July 31st *"Wrist better. Received Red Cross rations with some additional clothing. Not so quiet now. Further supply of drugs from Nips. No more yet nor likely. No diarrhoea. Inclined to be testy."*

August 11th *"Have diarrhoea again rather severe. Know I still have ascaris. Smoking reasonably well. Have a bad cardiac beri-beri case but he has heartened this morning. This diary is almost complete I think."*

* * * * *

This is a cryptic reference to a whole series of conditions and events. We had had 'pirate' radios for the whole of the captivity and had had almost continuous access to them. News generally came from Delhi Radio; was listened to in conditions of extreme danger and then recounted to one of the 'watchdogs' who helped to guard the safety of the radio listener. He would memorise it and then quietly pass it on to the person in a hut most likely to have a reliable memory and complete discretion. Each man only knew his two contacts up and down so to speak. Groups of men would then gather closely together while the gist of the news was passed on. It is obvious that the system led to some strange reports at the end of the line but comparison with the occupants of other huts helped to produce an 'average' bulletin which was near the truth.

On 6th August 1945, the first atomic bomb was dropped on Hiroshima but the news from Delhi was vague and uncertain and it did not reach the prisoners. There followed the dropping of the second atomic bomb on Nagasaki. We were told (a few of us only) that there had been this unknown type of enormous bomb dropped, and on 14th or 15th August we were told about the unconditional surrender of Japan.

We knew therefore that the end of the war was at hand if only we could hang on. The wonder was that for ten days from 11th August to 21st the whole camp of prisoners knew about the bombs, and the surrender, but no one said a word to the guards. Wisely, because many Japanese units had decided on no surrender and on a policy of massacre of the prisoners; resistance till death, or hara-kiri. This is reflected in the entry for September 6th.

However to refer back to the bad cardiac beri-beri case we had. I cannot recall his name but he had been suffering from 'wet' beri-beri for weeks. In other words his body had bloated with oedema due to the vitamin B1 deficiency. There was no medication which would help. He had had to suffer the trocha and canula treatment [a system of stabbing a hole and draining off large quantities of fluid] but within days the water returned. He lay on a bamboo 'cot' — deliberately made to be about three feet off the floor to aid in nursing, and he was almost as high as he was long — that is, his abdomen was distended to a height of feet above the bed. This is no exaggeration. I couldn't see over him! Naturally he was in a terminal condition. At any time his heart which had already indicated that the strain was telling would simply stop. He lay in a stupor next to coma. He did not speak; we did not know whether he slept or not; he had given up.

On the day it was certain that if we could only hang on we would be freed I spent a lot of time — I don't know how long, almost shouting into his ear that we were going to be free; that something stupendous had happened to make it possible for him to receive treatment; to live. The second day I spoke to him he said, simply 'yes' and I knew I had won. Like a miracle, without medication, his weight went down, he began urinating again under his own power — he started to eat the better food which came along. He walked out of the camp as fit as any of us. This I believe to be the third most striking instance I had whilst a prisoner, of the power of the mind over the body. He decided to live, and came back from the edge of the grave.

* * * * *

August 21st *"On 18th Yoshikawa Socho, the camp Commandant, told Major Bradshaw our OC that a negotiated peace was taking place. The war was at an end and our own people would soon be taking over. Since then the wire between the two camps has been taken down. The rice ration has increased to 500 grammes per day and we hear rumours of good food. We have been daily expecting Lord Louis to come for us but he delays. There are interesting things happening all the time. Important staff cars on the road. Cessations of working parties. Cessation of all IJA fatigues. Release of all canteen goods. I am on a special diet because I am allergic to maize. Cheiropompholyx of the hands. Peeling scrotum etc. The IJA still guard us. Grand to see the lights on without shades. The Nips made a big issue of boots."*

Special Orders

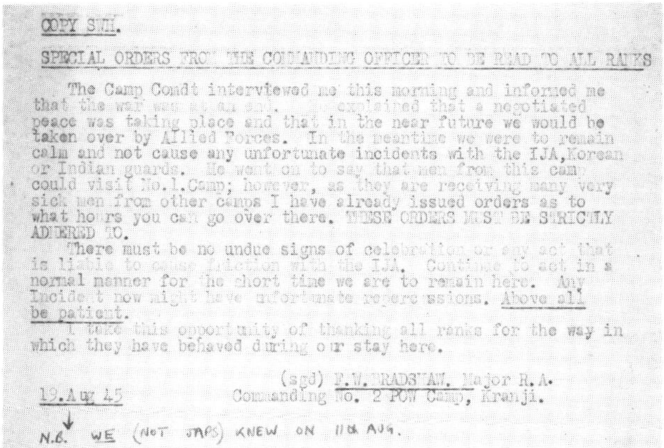

COPY SWI.

SPECIAL ORDERS FROM THE COMMANDING OFFICER TO BE READ TO ALL RANKS

The Camp Comdt interviewed me this morning and informed me that the war was at an end. He explained that a negotiated peace was taking place and that in the near future we would be taken over by Allied Forces. In the meantime we were to remain calm and not cause any unfortunate incidents with the IJA, Korean or Indian guards. He went on to say that men from this camp could visit No.1.Camp; however, as they are receiving many very sick men from other camps I have already issued orders as to what hours you can go over there. THESE ORDERS MUST BE STRICTLY ADHERED TO.

There must be no undue signs of celebration or any act that is liable to cause friction with the IJA. Continue to act in a normal manner for the short time we are to remain here. Any Incident now might have unfortunate repercussions. Above all be patient.

I take this opportunity of thanking all ranks for the way in which they have behaved during our stay here.

(sgd) F.W. BRADSHAW. Major R.A.
Commanding No. 2 POW Camp, Kranji.

19.Aug 45

N.B. WE (NOT JAPS) KNEW ON 11th AUG.

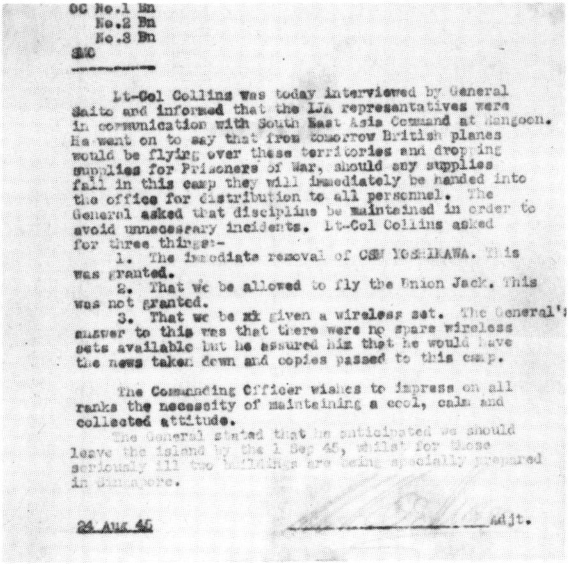

OC No.1 Bn
No.2 Bn
No.3 Bn
SMC

Lt-Col Collins was today interviewed by General Saito and informed that the IJA representatives were in communication with South East Asia Command at Rangoon. He went on to say that from tomorrow British planes would be flying over these territories and dropping supplies for Prisoners of War, should any supplies fall in this camp they will immediately be handed into the offices for distribution to all personnel. The General asked that discipline be maintained in order to avoid unnecessary incidents. Lt-Col Collins asked for three things:-

1. The immediate removal of CSM YOSHIKAWA. This was granted.
2. That we be allowed to fly the Union Jack. This was not granted.
3. That we be xx given a wireless set. The General's answer to this was that there were no spare wireless sets available but he assured him that he would have the news taken down and copies passed to this camp.

The Commanding Officer wishes to impress on all ranks the necessity of maintaining a cool, calm and collected attitude.

The General stated that he anticipated we should leave the island by the 1 Sep 45, whilst for those seriously ill two buildings are being specially prepared in Singapore.

24 Aug 45 ______________ Adjt.

16 *The Rising Sun Sets*

LIEUTENANT Wakabiashi sat in the lotus position on the little square rush mat he kept for his private devotions. He was a devout man and believed he came from Ancient Samurai stock. He had sworn, and meant with all his being, absolute fealty and obedience to his Sun-god, King Emperor Hirohito — The titular head of the Imperial Japanese Army. He believed unshakeably in the dogma that to surrender was dishonourable in any circumstances and merited death. To die in battle was the most glorious fate and wafted the fortunate warrior to be immediately with his ancestors in paradise.

As he sat he was unaware of the increasing cramp in his tightly crossed legs or that the long night would soon be over. He wore his white ceremonial robe and his short ceremonial sword lay across his knees. His hair was held back by a white headband; his eyes looked into space beyond the palm frond walls of his Quarters.

He remembered vividly his days at Oxford and the First Class Honours Degree he had obtained in English and History. He recalled his return to Kyoto and his entry into the army in honour of his recently dead father, through the halls of the Military Academy. He fought again the battles in China; he thought about the brief spell with the occupation troops in Korea; then the Malayan campaign and later a short spell in Siam. For the longest time he went over in his mind his tenure of office as Camp Commandant for prisoner-of-war camps. He tasted again the pleasure he had had discussing Shakespeare with one of the English prisoners and playing chess. He examined his conscience to be sure that he had done his duty. He did not realise or comprehend that many of his actions were regarded as cruel and barbaric. He considered the dreadful shame that had come upon the army and the nation because of the surrender to the allies; He could not, would not think shamefully of his Emperor, but he could at least gain honour in leaving this life.

Now the dawn was breaking and in a very few minutes the sun would be up. There came to him his Sergeant Major to tell him his 'guests' (some Officers and Warrant Officers who had been his prisoners) were outside waiting. He signed for them to come in and for the Gunso to stay. They formed a circle round him except for the space immediately in front of him.

He bowed his head in meditation, then picked up the ceremonial short sword, holding it reversed with two hands, and the point against his abdomen; he plunged it in, with superhuman will pulled it down and across; and as required fell forward on his face, his hands spread. The witnesses filed out.

By proper ceremonial, attired correctly, with a sanctified sword, and all the proper movements even in death, honour had come by hara kiri to Lieutenant Wakabiashi.

August 22nd *"Ration issues are very large. Rumours that Prince Chichibu came here, that the signing for this peace is today or tomorrow. Today received Red Cross parcels, one between two. The Nips appear to be getting rid of their surplus stock probably for self protection."*

* * * * *

One would think this would make everything right but it was a mixed blessing. Our metabolism had become used to dirty rice, bits of gristle, primitive green stuff and so on and the intake of European food, rich in fat, carbohydrates, protein, and vitamins was sometimes too much. We were warned to be careful; to mix small portions of the Red Cross parcel contents into our rice — to ease ourselves from one diet to the other. Many did not heed the advice and ate too heartily of the new food. At best this simply caused agonising digestion pains, or violent cramps and diarrhoea — at worst it caused deaths. One man, whom I begged not to do it, ate a whole twelve oz tin of corned beef on its own. He died within twelve hours.

* * * * *

August 26th *"Have received second Red Cross parcel of meat issue; 2 oz. for two days. Heaps of new clothing, mostly civilian, poor stuff. General Shaito told Colonel Collins on 24th that our people would be here soon. We asked for wireless set but could not get one! Impromptu concert last night. Having good time with Indians and Yoshikawa removed. Our men patrol the wire expecting planes."*

August 30th *"Nips are supplying small amounts of cheese, soya beans, some meat, pineapple and a few cigarettes. We live a lot better therefore, but not much. Lots of cases of oedema but not serious. They seem out to kill us with kindness. On 28th a Liberator flew low over the camp and dropped leaflet instructions in Japanese. They dropped one in English on another camp yesterday. Today we hear six people have landed from outside. We have British bugle calls now. I am off duty* *with a very heavy cold and general feeling of discomfort. This has been a very long three weeks."*

September 1st *"Time runs on. It's three weeks now and it seems as though we'll never get out. The Chinese gave the volunteers a pig yesterday and they gave it to the camp. One thousandth of a pig each. More Red Cross parcels today. We think two of the six people who landed on the 29th came in yesterday. Very young. Grand to see them. One says we shall probably go straight home without being delayed in India. It cannot be too soon. Small issue of butter and cigarettes yesterday. More planes over. All Korean guards taken away. Some civilian Eurasians visited the camp."*

September 4th *"Passed fairly quietly for these days although things are happening all the time. Had two concerts on the square. The flag has been hoisted. The canary will soon be on view. We are being given a big radio set. More troops and supplies have been dropped. Malays and Chinese Communists are fighting on the island. At eleven o'clock this morning naval units arrived. We believe 10th is deadline. We all have reasonable kit now. Excitement is high. Lot of Nips rations. Some guerrillas have come in. Had retreat blown tonight. Six years yesterday the War started."*

September 6th 1945 *"Many things happened today. Three news reporters came, one a woman — the first white woman! More paratroopers visited us including a young RAMC Lieutenant who had quite good news. Occupational troops Gurkas took over the camp today. The Nips have been leaving the island steadily for forty-eight hours. They must now realise the extent of their defeat. Rations are slightly better. Had open air concert tonight. Expect to start embarking about Sunday. Hope to be home soon. Am quite fit. Learnt today that in the event of an invasion we were to be massacred and that the invasion forces left Rangoon on the 11th but our people knew and were going to drop paratroops in the hope of saving 50% of us."*

September 7th *"British Movietone News took some pictures. I managed to get in one. Free distribution of English cigarettes. I got some. Had talk with woman war correspondent. Had talk with a Lance Corporal from an Indian field ambulance."*

September 10th *"8th quiet. 9th went on pass into Singapore. Walked 'till tired. Saw hospital ships and HMS Sussex. The Chinese gave us aerated waters. Naval Police gave us English cigarettes. Hitched-hiked both ways. Good day but tiring. Royal Marines' band came up today for half-an-hour. No news of move. Very good to see Nips working."*

September 17th *"A lot has happened. Lord Louis came to see us some days ago, a great man. Yesterday had another day in town. Heard of conditions in England.*

Went to Naval base on 15th to search Nips. Took some stuff from them. Today my birthday. I expect to embark."

* * * * *

This was the last entry in the diary because my name did come up and at one hour's notice (about fifty-nine minutes more than was needed) I clambered on to a lorry to go to the docks, and ran into what was perhaps for me the strangest episode of my army life. The reader will have gathered that I did not suffer fools gladly, tended to be a bit rebellious and was no great respecter of persons; primarily because I found among the full-time serving officers and other ranks of the day a good deal of stupidity, and a good deal of contempt for the volunteer or conscript soldier who in the end carried the can. We arrived at the docks, myself and many of the sergeants who had been working for and with me. We were met on that sunlit quayside by a pompous Lieutenant and his Sergeant Major, who had spent most of the war 'trooping' on board ship — never in dangerous waters, and always with the best of conditions, who thought that prisoners-of-war would be fawningly grateful for anything. I was allotted a 'bedspace' and my sergeants were allotted 'deck numbers'. I smelt a rat but went up the gangway. I found I had been allotted accommodation according to regulations for sergeants in peace time, and that my sergeants were slinging hammocks with everybody else in overcrowded conditions for everybody. Of course they had been our companions, for some years but I couldn't see why the regular serving troops should have better accommodation than we did. So I led my first and last mutiny. I took all my sergeants back down the gangplank; explained to the 'thick' trooping officers that we were no longer prisoners-of-war; and that we were entitled to certain conditions under King's Regulations; and that they knew what they could do with their ship; we were not budging off the quay until we got our rights — even if it meant another three years!

It worked — we had our rights and there was a marked change in the attitude of the trooping staff to the ex-prisoners from then on.

We travelled via Colombo, the Suez Canal, with a brief stop at Gibraltar. The ship was the 'Nieuw Amsterdam' still being run by Dutch merchant marines and they were marvellous. They treated us like heroes and overruled any petty restriction the authorities tried to place on us. Apart from the bridge we were allowed to go anywhere on the ship and mingle freely. They fed us superbly — so much so that in the twenty-nine days the ship took to get to Liverpool most of us gained weight to the tune of about one pound per day — in my own case exactly two stones in the month.

So on a foggy morning not quite four years from departure I arrived back in England.

17 *The painful return 1945/46*

THAT should have been the end of the uncertainty, the ordeal and the pain, but strangely it was not.

We came back to a world different from that of nearly four years ago. Rationing and austerity had bitten deep into the fabric of society. Attitudes towards ex-prisoners-of-war were ambivalent — some welcoming us, if not as heroes at least as people to be cherished, whilst others turned their backs and wanted us not to say anything, or do anything just to go away and not bother them.

It was a month after the ending of the War with Japan, and four months since the tremendous celebrations of V.E. day. There was a new kind of government, and the corridors of power did not want to know about such dirty words as compensation, or squeezing recompense out of our previous captors for the indignities and suffering we had experienced.

I first felt the 'difference' as soon as we had been dumped by army trucks at the Liverpool railway station. We were ordinary travellers. Bored station staff were not bothered whether we found a train or not, and looked suspiciously at our brand new uniforms (issued in Ceylon) and our lack of medal ribbons, (The War Office did not get around to this for months), but we found the train and arrived in London after a tedious journey lasting all day.

There, embarrassingly, W.V.S. ladies descended upon us, knowing we were coming, insisted on hefting our baggage and took us to whichever Army truck was due to transfer us to our next railway station. The ride was one of the happiest of my life. Through darkened London, with street lights shining and down roads very familiar to me from having worked there before the war.

Our numbers had of course dwindled as we dispersed and there were just three of us who boarded a train at Victoria for Brighton. That journey too was exciting, since for some years I had commuted on the line between Brighton and London and seeing old landmarks gave a stimulus to my low spirits.

I was about halfway down the train so had about 50 yards or more to walk to the barrier. I could see my (then) wife and a girl who had to be my daughter, but it wasn't until I was within a few feet that I recognised the 9 year old I had left behind when she was 5.

In those days taxis and petrol were scarce but a man approached us and said he guessed I was a returned prisoner-of-war and could he take us home. On the journey, through the familiar Brighton streets he leaned over his seat and gave me two eggs. I was not surprised when he refused to be paid on arrival — what did surprise me was that people should make so much fuss about two eggs — until the awful strictures of rationing were borne in upon me. Parents and parents-in-law were in the house to greet me and it was then I realised how difficult life was going to be in the immediate future. Meeting people — especially those who went out of their way to be kind and — yes — loving was an agony.

For weeks tears would come to my eyes and I could not speak when meeting again old friends and relations. If they put on a welcome home party I was completely overcome. They thought I was surly and could not understand why I wanted to talk and talk about my experiences. They prevented me.

Even at home the subject was taboo but I had to let it out. I would wake in the small hours accustomed as we had been for so many years to this routine, drenched with sweat from nightmares unbelievable.

It really was inevitable. For four years one had lived on one's nerves. It had been impossible to break down for that way lay madness or even death. One didn't 'go sick' because to admit that one felt poorly was to succumb to whatever diabolical complaint had hold of you. I particularly would not give in, having always been a stubborn-minded individual. I had been determined to see the thing through — from sheer cussedness and possibly cowardice, because I did not want my life to be ruined by an accident of politics. I had had to see disease, injury and death sufficient to fill a normal nurses lifetime twice over: I had to minister to the sick and dying, and be hard about it because compassion though outward, could not be always inward because it meant breakdown.

We had for years jeered at misfortune, shrugged at bad news; we had sunk spiritually as low as any man could; physically we had endured an encyclopaedia of illnesses and by our spirit mostly, overcame them.

I had had dengue fever I think twice; Benign tertian malaria more or less continuously on and off — although perhaps it could be counted as something up to sixteen acute attacks; I had had malign tertian malaria and been out of my mind for two days, hovering on permanent madness: I had even had cholera, which, in those circumstances, no man endured for more than one day and lived; tropical ulcers, cheiropomphlyx, tinea of feet and scrotum, dry beri-beri were our constant companions; some had had operations — I had had an anal fistula repaired. Throughout it all there was dysentery as an endemic disease, recurring and recurring; worm infestation, and of course, complete wasting from malnutrition and avitaminosis. One could go on. The gruesome list is merely to emphasise how much we had had to rely on our spirit, or for those with a Faith in their beliefs and prayers as well.

Only the mental process, the *will* to live prevented thousands more dying than did. But it all cost a huge sum in drawing on nervous energy.

What I needed, and many like me, was to pour out our hearts to those close to us — to rid ourselves of the poisons of emotions. For those who like myself were denied this catharsis, mental recovery was delayed and impaired, almost permanently.

Today I cannot bear people to be kind to me, particularly as a surprise, without some (what probably appears foolish) demonstration of emotion.

Thus it was that in spite of six months demobilisation leave, and double ration books, and making myself busy trying to get published the novels I had written as a prisoner, I went back to my job on the last day possible, and having reached Victoria, could not face it and got straight back on the train.

A week later (after a convenient 'indisposition') I braved re-entry to the world of business. I found that true I had a job back, but I had lost about ten places in the promotion race mostly to those who had stayed behind with flat feet or very poor vision, or 'reserved occupations'. Moreover I was really rather a nuisance coming back at all.

So I studied hard and within two years had qualified and changed to a totally different job. I had had one of my novels published; it was only then I felt that I had returned and had a future to look forward to.

* * * * *

After the end of the War there had to be a re-birth — painful but eventually joyous.

We have a Far East Prisoners of War Association — their motto is 'To keep going the Spirit that kept us going' — a trite saying but so very, very true.

THE END AND THE BEGINNING

Appendix

S.S. Empress of Asia

(Extract from 'Histories of Individual Ships' by courtesy of C.P. Ships)

The *Empress of Asia* started trooping to the Near East in April 1941, leaving Liverpool and sailing via Freetown, Cape Town and Durban to reach Suez on the 24 June. On leaving Port Said on 29 June 1941, Donald Smith, the chief officer, invited two young naval officers who were returning to England to sit at his table. One was Prince Philip of Greece, who travelled as far as Durban and there transferred to the *Empress of Russia*.

In company with the *Empress of Japan* II and with 2235 troops in addition to her crew of 416, she left Liverpool on 12 November 1941, sailing via Cape Town and Bombay. She arrived off Singapore on 4 February 1942. The *Empress* had the stern position in the convoy through the Banka Strait on the east coast of Sumatra. Captain J. B. Smith, with reference to the *Asia*'s place at the end of the line, reported somewhat dryly: 'We had been allotted this position on account of our steaming difficulties, the ship almost invariably dropping astern of station when fires were being cleaned.' In a later interview Captain Smith explained:

> Well-trained Chinese firemen got the best out of the two coal burners from the Pacific Fleet, but by the time World War II broke out there was a real dearth of firemen accustomed to coal and after our Chinese firemen returned home we had to rely on what the Merchant Seamen's Pools could scrape up.

At 11am on 4 February the convoy was sighted by Japanese aircraft and a few near misses damaged two of her lifeboats. At the same time on the following morning the official report shows that:

> A large formation of Japanese aircraft passed overhead and disappeared in the clouds. Later they reappeared, seemingly coming from all directions and flying at both high and low altitudes. All ships in the convoy, including the escorting light cruiser and a sloop, opened fire. Bombs started falling all round the *Empress* and it was evident that the ship had been singled out to bear the brunt of the attack.

A stick of bombs scored the first hits, one going through the ornate dome over the lounge. A second bomb pierced the lounge and destroyed the radio equipment. Other bombs caused much damage to the engine room, including the auxiliary power plants, fractured pipes in the interior of the ship and started many fires. The chief officer reported that bombs had penetrated all decks, smoke and flames hindering attempts to control the fires which by 11.25am were out of control. The captain's report continues:

> At this time we were passing between minefields to the North and South of the swept channel. I decided to swing the ship round and anchor close to the Sultan Shoal Lighthouse. At this time it was impossible to remain on the Bridge any longer on account of the smoke and heat.

One happy feature of the Japanese concentration on the *Empress of Asia* was that the other less badly damaged ships were able to get small boats away when the *Empress* was abandoned, thus keeping the loss of life to a minimum. The Australian sloop *Yarra* came alongside aft and took off well over a thousand troops and crew. By 1pm all personnel were off the ship. A later check showed fifteen military unaccounted for and one member of the crew dead as a result of injuries sustained in the bombing.

The deck and engine-room crew were later posted by the naval authorities to various small coastal ships to help in the evacuation of Singapore. Many of the catering staff volunteered for duty in Singapore hospitals and were later interned by the Japanese. Recognition of her service by HM the King was expressed in the award of the OBE to Captain J. B. Smith, the MBE to First Officer L. H. Johnston and a mention in dispatches for Chief Officer Donald Smith.

During World War II the *Asia* travelled 46,993 miles, carried 6839 troops, 1000 prisoners of war, eighty-four civilians and 3495 tons of cargo.

Medical Reports

These are transcripts taken from the annual medical reports of the Prisoner-of-War Camp, Changi, from 15th February, 1942 to 15th February, 1945, as prepared by the Medical Officers concerned at the time and later submitted to the War Office but eventually not printed or published and intended to be destroyed. The wording of this report is in fact taken from the carbon copies of the original report which was saved by a member of the staff of the Ministry at the time. The whole thing is prefaced with the title page 'GHQ 2486'.

This is an extract from the Annual Medical Report (February 1942 to February 1943)

1. (i) *Camp area*

The *Changi POW* camp is located at the East corner of Singapore island and is bounded on the North by the Johore Straits and on the East and South by the sea and the Western boundary wire runs exclusive Loyang camp inclusive road Loyang camp Tampenis road junction of Tampenis and Changi Roads — inclusive road from Provost Camp — Tamar Merahbesar. The ground within the area consists of low undulating laterite hills interspaced with swamp and sand. It is well wooded with coconut and rubber predominating and much of the swampy foreshore is covered with mangrove, the ubiquitous grass is halang. The climate is healthy, rainfall averaging about 100″ to 120″ annually. There is no actual dry season but at two periods throughout the year, that is March to May and October to November precipitation is above normal. Shade temperatures show little variation maximum being 94° and minimum 80° Fahrenheit. Humidity ranges from 75% to 90%.

On the higher ground within the area are located Kitchener, Roberts and Gordon Barracks. The Royal Artillery Wayward, Birdwood and India lines the various messes, Officers bungalows and married quarters pertaining thereto and Changi village. This accommodation was constructed to house one brigade.

All light soil from the buildings was disposed of by water carriers to septic tanks into the sea. Sullage water was removed in open concrete drains. The water supply was obtained by gravity feed from the Singapore Municipal Supply. Booster pumps being employed locally to carry it to the higher levels of Changi.

(ii) *Conditions on arrival*

Changi was heavily bombed during the hostilities. The damage to buildings was not as severe as it might have been but the sewage system and the water supply had been put out of action. In addition on evacuation by ourselves, the R.E. workshop, the water pumps, the electric lighting had been destroyed. Into this area between 17th and 20th February, 1942 were crowded some 47,000 British prisoners, the Indian troops being completely segregated at Nee Soon. The troops marched out the 17 miles from Singapore un-escorted with a minimum of kit and equipment. They found sanitary arrangements non-existent and flies already prevalent. Water was available in the mains in very limited quantities in the lower levels only and this with the output of four anti-malarial drains formed the only sources of supply; it accordingly had to be rationed at ½ gallon per head daily for all purposes. Until the I.J.A. ration became available on 24th February, food was limited to such as the troops had been able to bring with them.

The mental reaction of the troops to the capitulation was severe, morale was low and inertia general. There were therefore all the predisposing factors for the major epidemic of dysentery which commenced within a few days of arrival and resulted in 16,000 cases.

(iii) *Further course of events*

The main hospital was opened in Robert Barracks on the 24th February in very cramped quarters and all subsidiary hospitals were closed with the exception of the Australian which was maintained for a time at Selarang and later amalgamated with the Roberts Hospital under instructions received from the I.J.A. The gross overcrowding, the limited water supply and the absence of artificial lighting, the lack of proper means of sewage disposal and the shortage of stores and equipment, in conjunction with a high admittance rate before organisation was complete, all presented enormous difficulties of administration in the early days.

The troops after a slow start gradually became fly conscious and settled down to cleaning up the area and the construction of efficient field sanitary works. Cook houses were improvised and much effort put into the construction of fly proof latrines and Otway pits and the adoption of anti-fly measures in general. The digging of deep bores and trenches and the proper disposal of refuse did much to eliminate the fly menace, but the work was much handicapped by lack of tools, earth augers and materials for fly proof tops. However, by these means and after much labour, the dysentery epidemic was eventually brought under control.

Vigorous anti-malarial measures were adopted from the commencement and at no time did the disease get out of hand.

These labours together with the felling and chopping of timber for fuel, the construction of gardens and normal unit fatigues kept the men occupied.

Overcrowding was at first extreme but later the worst was relieved by the transfer of large numbers of troops in April and May to Singapore where they were located in the various camps and employed in cleaning up the destruction caused by the bombardment; there were duties around the docks and elsewhere. Keeping in touch with these camps was difficult and spasmodic and none at all was possible with the Indian Camp at Nee Soon.

At first all troops had full freedom within the camp area but later formations were wired off separately within the confines of their respective barracks and all intercommunication controlled by the I.J.A. through a system of flags and sentries. The troops soon adapted themselves to their environment but the rations supplied by the I.J.A. were quite inadequate in many respects for the preservation of health. As a result a severe outbreak of beriberi commenced in April followed in June by the various manifestations associated with deficiences of other factors of the Vitamin B complex. The former was in course of time largely eliminated but the latter remained an insoluble problem for the rest of the year except for a brief period in October and November when Red Cross stores were available but further complication was added by a sharp outbreak of diphtheria in August, treatment of which was much handicapped by lack of serum.

Matters were not helped early in September by a concentration of all troops in Changi except the hospital at Selarang Square for four days as a punishment for refusing to sign parole. 14,000 troops were herded into an area intended for one battalion without food and with the minimum of water. A special report of this incident is attached as an annex. Much attention was given to keeping the minds of the troops occupied. A University embracing many subjects was commenced, art and cookery exhibitions were held, and concerts, theatricals and games organised. It was not long before the morale of the troops was fully re-established. In addition gardens were opened up, piggery commenced and poultry keeping encouraged in an effort to supplement the inadequate diet.

In April private purchase of sundry articles specified by the Japanese became possible through an Indian contractor appointed to the camp (Gian Singh) of the local purchase for the hospital was permitted. In those days also while individuals still possessed private funds there was a flourishing black market over the wall with the local Chinese. Canteens were started and bulk local purchase commenced in June with an amenity grant Officers 25 cents, NCOs 15 cents and Privates 10 cents per day was made available by the I.J.A. Articles so purchaseable were, however, limited. In September Officers first received pay and it then became possible to establish, hospital, camp and messing funds.

Changes in personnel began in April when a party of 1125 left for unknown destinations overseas. These were followed by 3,000 in May and another 3,000 in June and 3,600 in July mainly by the overland route. In August all Senior Officers including the DDMS and the majority of his staff were transferred overseas. Further parties left overland in October and from the beginning of that month Changi was utilised by the I.J.A. as a transit camp and bodies of troops from the Dutch East Indies were continually arriving and departing after a brief stay either up overseas or up country. The sanitation of these parties left much to be desired and was a constant source of anxiety.

This is an extract from the Annual Medical Report (February 1944 to February 1945)

No sooner, however, was this organisation completed than on 25th April, 1944 orders were received for the concentration of all POWs at the Changi jail by the end of May. An exception was made with regard to the hospital the main portion of which was detailed to proceed to an unknown destination (which eventually proved to be *Woodlands Camp, Karanji)* and the minor portion of which was to proceed with the troops to the jail. At this time the jail was occupied by the civil internees and the first step in the move was to the change over of H Force at Sime Road by the 9th. The rear party of F Force 600 strong which had recently arrived at Singapore from Thailand also accompanied H Force.

Meanwhile the move of the main hospital to Karanji proceeded smoothly by lorry, the advance party leaving on the 19th May followed by the main body from the 25th onwards; by the 28th this move was complete. The move of the remainder to the jail was completed on the last day of May. The hospital at Karanji was predominantly British in character whilst that at the jail was predominantly Australian.

Meanwhile the hospital at Karanji had settled in satisfactorily entirely separate and self contained unit, the function of which was defined by the I.J.A. as treatment of the chronic medical cases and the selected surgical. Inter-transfers with Karanji took place weekly and at the end of September when moves were limited to thrice monthly.

Proteins appeared to be the main lack felt by the troops and the cat and dog population of the camps steadily diminished. Pythons, Cobras, snails and frogs, sparrows and even rats and lizards were not despised by some enterprising individuals who reported favourably on their palatability and nourishing properties.

Explanation of March Route

The stages on the railway and the halts on the road sometimes had names shown on local maps; sometimes there were inhabitants from there or thereabouts who had a name for the place; sometimes even there were tiny villages. From all these sources the Japanese made 'official' names of places; the local inhabitants made theirs and the soldiery twisted the unfamiliar words to make them pronounceable in English.

For these reasons each place often had more than one 'name'. A recognised expert in this field is Geoffrey Pharaoh Adams, author of 'No time for Geishas', who has produced one of the most definitive lists published in several places reproduced and drawn by C. E. Escritt in 'After the Battle' No. 26 published by Battle of Britain Prints International Ltd. in 1979. There are others however including one by Lt. Col. A. A. Johnson MC of the 4th Battn. Suffolk Regiment which was bound into his publication of Flora and Fauna painted by Allied Prisoners in Siam published by the Sladmore Gallery. There were others who produced duplicated drawings and in particular there is an Official Report on Conditions of Prisoners of War in Thailand May-Dec 1943, which contained a sketch map with names and distances.

The following map printed in this book, and the schematic route with names and distances derives from all these and notes taken by the Author (see also page 56). To all these authors, publishers, and others, who may have helped to supply the information used the Author acknowledges his indebtedness and recognises their rights, as he hopes they will recognise his.

THE ROUTE OF THE MARCH – TO BE READ FROM BOTTOM UP – TO MATCH WITH MAP

JAPANESE STAGES ON RAILWAY (Author's numbers)		kilometres from 'base' camp	Names of halts on road march with alternate (village) names: Diary and Map reference Nos.		Miles covered on each stage with cumulative total	Date reached 1943
	HERE IS THREE PAGODAS PASS – THE FRONTIER BETWEEN THAILAND AND BURMA					
36	Sonkurai (Kaung Kluài)	299.02	Son Krai	(18)	3 (191)	Aug 2
			Shimo Son Krai		5 (191)	
35	Nieke (Nikki)	281.80	Nieke	(17)	2 (186)	Jul 11
			Lower Nieke (Shimo Nikki)	(16)	2 (184)	May 18
			Upper Teimonta	(15)	2½(182)	May 17
34	Teimonta (Timantar)	273.06			3¼(179½)	
			Upper Koncuita	(14)	3¼(175¼)	May 16
	Here at	262.87	the two halves of the railway track met			
33	Konkoita (Koncuita)	262.58	Koncuita	(13)	(172)	May 15
32	Kurikonta	257.70			15	
31	Kurian kurai (Kreung Krai)	250.13				
30	Tamoranpato (Tamuran Part)	244.19	Tampranpat	(12)	(157)	May 14
29	Tamazayou (Tomajo)	236.80			16	
28	Namuchonyai (Namjo)	222.14				
27	Takanun (Dha Khanun)	218.15	Tarkamoon	(11)	(141)	May 13
					11	
26	Purankashii (Brankassi)	208.11	Broncali (Prongpari)	(10)	(130)	May 11
25	Hindato (Hin Dat)	197.75			13	
			Wompin(village)	(9)	(117)	May 10
24	Kuiie (Kui Ye)	190.48			14	
23	Rinten (Rintin)	180.53				
22	Kinsaiyoku (Kinsaiyok)(Main camp)	171.72	Kinsayo	(8)	(103)	May 8
21	Saiyoku (sub-camp) (Village)	167.66			12	
20	Kannyui (Kanu)	162.30	Kenyui	(7)	(91)	May 7
19	Hintoku (Hintok)	155.03				
18	Tampi (Tampines)	147.52			14	
17	Tonchan	139.05				
16	Tasoe (Tha Soe)	130.30	Tahso	(6)	(77)	May 6
	This is now called NAMTOK – railway from Bampong ends here 1976					
15	Wanyai (Wung Yai)(village)	124.84				
14	Wampo (Wang Po)	114.04			15	
13	Aruhiru (Arrow Hill)	108.14				
			Wonyon (village)	(5)	(62)	May 4
12	Takiren (Tarkilen)(village)	97.89				
11	Bankao	87.89			15	
10	Tapon	77.66				
9	Wanyan (Wan Hain)	68.59				
			Wompah	(4)	(47)	May 3
8	Kaopon (Chungkai)	57.30			15	
	Here is the bridge over the Mae Klaeung river – incorrectly called the Kwae					
7	Kanchanabri (Canburi)	50.32	Kanburi	(3)	(32)	May 1
6.	Tamoan (Tha Muang)	38.90			15	
5	Taruanoi	25.89	Torowa	(2)	(17)	April 30
4	Rukke	13.38				
3	Bampommai (Banpong)	5.13	Banpong	(1)		April 28
2	Komma	2.00			17	
1	Nompuradokku (Nong Pladuk)	–	Nonpraduk	(1A)		April 29
	Large staging camp after debarking from the railway from Singapore.					

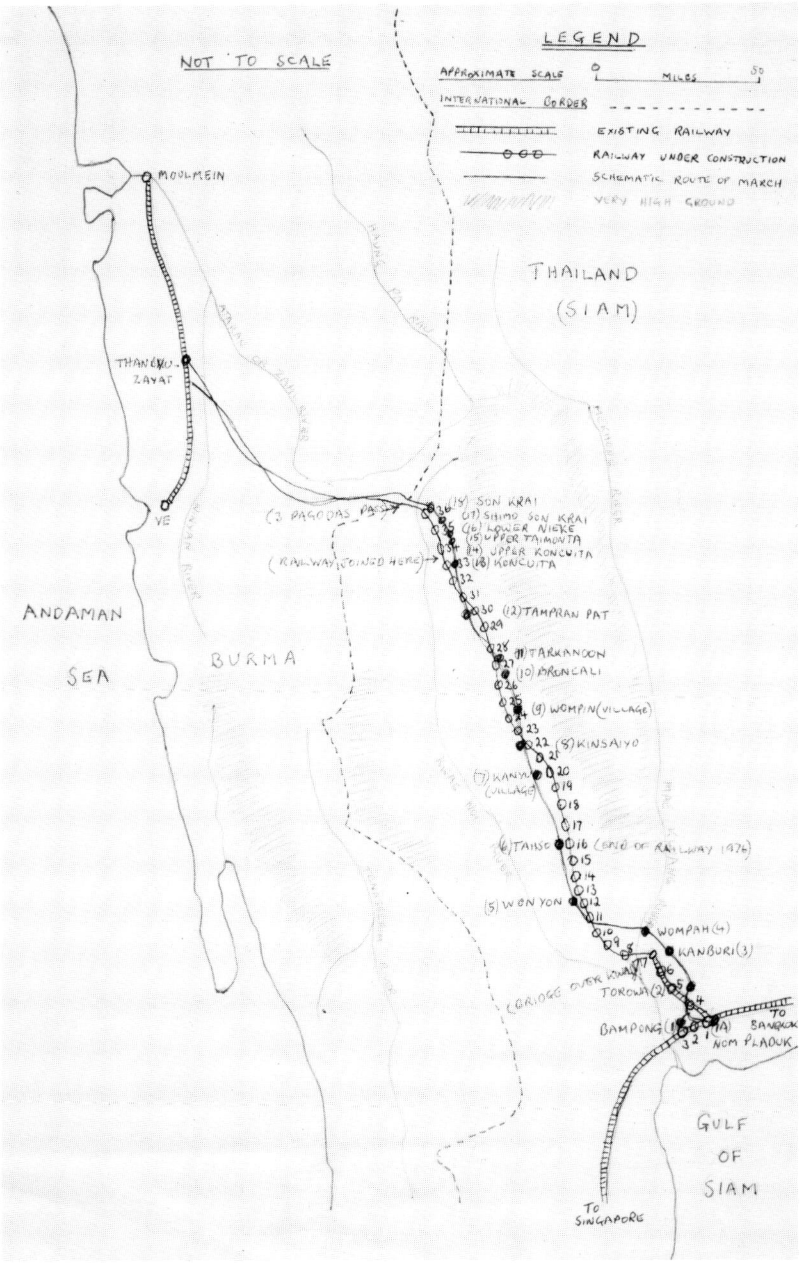
NOT TO SCALE
LEGEND
APPROXIMATE SCALE 0 MILES 50
INTERNATIONAL BORDER
EXISTING RAILWAY
RAILWAY UNDER CONSTRUCTION
SCHEMATIC ROUTE OF MARCH
VERY HIGH GROUND
MOULMEIN
THANBYUZAYAT
YE
THAILAND
(SIAM)
ANDAMAN
SEA
BURMA
(3 PAGODAS PASS)
(RAILWAY JOINED HERE)
(18) SON KRAI
(17) SHIMO SON KRAI
(16) LOWER NIEKE
(15) UPPER TAIMONTA
(14) UPPER KONCUITA
(13) KONCUITA
(12) TAMPRAN PAT
(11) TARKANOON
(10) BRONCALI
(9) WOMPIN (VILLAGE)
(8) KINSAIYO
(7) KANYU (VILLAGE)
(6) TAHSO
(END OF RAILWAY 1976)
(5) WON YON
WOMPAH (4)
KANBURI (3)
TOROWA (2)
(BRIDGE OVER KWAI)
BAMPONG (1)
(1A) NOM PLADUK
TO BANGKOK
GULF OF SIAM
TO SINGAPORE